Learning Drupal 8

D1332649

Create complex websites quickly and easily using the building blocks of Drupal 8, the most powerful version of Drupal yet

Nick Abbott

Richard Jones

BIRMINGHAM - MUMBAI

Learning Drupal 8

First published: January 2016

Production reference: 1270116

Published by Packt Publishing Ltd.
Livery Place
35 Livery Street
Birmingham B3 2PB, UK.

ISBN 978-1-78216-875-1

www.packtpub.com

Credits

Authors
Nick Abbott
Richard Jones

Reviewers
James Roughton
Tracy Charles Smith
Michelle Williamson

Commissioning Editor
Andrew Duckworth

Acquisition Editor
Richard Brookes-Bland

Content Development Editor
Dharmesh Parmar

Technical Editor
Anushree Arun Tendulkar

Copy Editor
Charlotte Carneiro

Project Coordinator
Mary Alex

Proofreader
Safis Editing

Indexer
Tejal Daruwale Soni

Production Coordinator
Melwyn Dsa

Cover Work
Melwyn Dsa

About the Authors

Nick Abbott is the head of training at iKOS. Nick started his digital life in 1981 working on an ICL 2904 mainframe, a Commodore PET, and a Commodore VIC20. After the ritual stint in BASIC, he moved on to writing games in Z80 and 6502 assemblers, hardware interfacing, and many happy hours creating business solutions with the BBC Micro based around the Acorn View family. Old but not obsolete. He graduated with a first class degree in applied physics in the late 1980s, and he worked in IT and education right up until he joined iKOS in 2008.

Richard Jones is the Technical Director and co-founder of iKOS (now part of the Inviqa group) — a European digital agency specializing in Drupal. Richard's first computer was an 8-bit BBC Master and this began his journey into computing proper. Indeed, his first introduction to working with Nick was by way of a school database project using the then legendary Acorn ViewStore package — way ahead of its time as an EPROM-based offering. He graduated with a first class degree in mechanical engineering in 1996 and has been working with various web technologies ever since.

They have both worked exclusively with Drupal on all their projects for 7 years. Richard and Nick have been collaborating on projects since the mid-1990s and have a great balance of skills between them that mean the first draft of collaborative work will have already been through many critical rewrites.

They both live in the Drupal ecosystem on a daily basis and *Getting Started with Drupal Commerce* — the first title they worked on with *Packt Publishing* — was well received.

About the Reviewers

James Roughton is an experienced safety professional with in-depth knowledge of the use of social media to help improve productivity. He is an accomplished speaker, author, and writer, and he develops and manages his own websites that provide a resource network for small businesses at http://safetycultureacademy.com/.

Three of his most notable books include *Safety Culture: An Innovative, Leadership Approach*, *Developing an Effective Safety Culture: A Leadership Approach*, and *Job Hazard Analysis: A Guide for Voluntary Compliance and Beyond*. He is an active board member and web master for the Georgia Conference — www.georgiaconference.org.

He was a President of the Georgia ASSE; Chair of Gwinnett Safety Professionals, and adjunct Professor of Safety Technology at Lanier Tech, Georgia Tech, and currently adjunct Professor at Columbia Southern University. He has received awards for his efforts and was named the Georgia Chapter ASSE Safety Professional of the Year 1998-1999. He also won the Project Safe Georgia award, 2008, and received the Georgia Safety, Health, and Environmental Conference's Earl Everett distinguished Service award, 2014.

Tracy Charles Smith is currently working as a project manager for Phase2, based out of Alexandria, Virginia. Tracy has experience in programming, database design, and project management. He has been developing web applications since 1999 and has used various languages and technologies including ColdFusion and PHP. Before becoming a project manager, Tracy was a senior developer working on large website implementations using Drupal as a platform.

In addition to reviewing Learning Drupal 8, Tracy authored *Drupal Intranets with Open Atrium* in 2011 and has reviewed several other books, including *ColdFusion 9 Developer Tutorial*. Tracy's entrepreneurial spirit has been a key component to Tracy's success in interacting with clients and team members on business and user-experience related technology solutions. In fact, he used that passion to start his own technology consulting firm called Alpha Geek Tech, LLC. He also served as a technology director for Quiddities Dev, Inc, in Santa Cruz, CA, before moving to the DC area to join Phase2. He earned a BS degree in computer information systems and business administration from Wingate University.

Michelle Williamson got her start in Drupal with version 5 and was immediately hooked by the learning curve and community. She currently works at Mediacurrent, a leading distributed Drupal agency, as Accessibility Lead. She spends her days building Drupal sites and making them more usable and friendly to people with disabilities. She is especially excited about the release of Drupal 8 and the various accessibility enhancements that come with it.

When not in front of a computer, Michelle is usually taking her puppies on hikes, cooking nutritious food, or has her nose in a Kindle.

www.PacktPub.com

Support files, eBooks, discount offers, and more

For support files and downloads related to your book, please visit www.PacktPub.com.

Did you know that Packt offers eBook versions of every book published, with PDF and ePub files available? You can upgrade to the eBook version at www.PacktPub.com and as a print book customer, you are entitled to a discount on the eBook copy. Get in touch with us at service@packtpub.com for more details.

At www.PacktPub.com, you can also read a collection of free technical articles, sign up for a range of free newsletters and receive exclusive discounts and offers on Packt books and eBooks.

https://www2.packtpub.com/books/subscription/packtlib

Do you need instant solutions to your IT questions? PacktLib is Packt's online digital book library. Here, you can search, access, and read Packt's entire library of books.

Why subscribe?

- Fully searchable across every book published by Packt
- Copy and paste, print, and bookmark content
- On demand and accessible via a web browser

Free access for Packt account holders

If you have an account with Packt at www.PacktPub.com, you can use this to access PacktLib today and view 9 entirely free books. Simply use your login credentials for immediate access.

Table of Contents

Preface

This book is designed to be an absolute beginners' step-by-step guide to learning Drupal 8.

Our aim was to write a book that explains what Drupal is and how to use it completely from scratch. We do not assume that the reader is familiar with any previous versions of Drupal, and we won't be referring to terms such as "Schema" and "MVC" in the assumption that the reader is necessarily already a web developer.

We have made every effort to keep the language as simple as humanly possible to illustrate every single step of the way so as to speed the would-be Drupal site builder on your way to building real state-of-the-art sites.

What this book covers

Chapter 1, *Introduction*, gives background information on Drupal and content management systems in general. Also some history on the Drupal project itself and how we got here.

Chapter 2, *Installation*, shows how to obtain a copy of Drupal 8 and install it on your own computer so you can get started on the rest of the chapters in this book.

Chapter 3, *Basic Concepts*, shows us each of the components to provide a better foundation for learning Drupal. This chapter also defines the terminology you will come across.

Chapter 4, *Getting Started with the UI*, walks you through the key parts of the standard Drupal 8 user interface (UI) focusing our on the Toolbar, the Administration menu and Shortcuts. This chapter is intended to provide you with a quick overview and much more detail and guided tutorial assignments will follow in later chapters.

Chapter 5, Basic Content, discusses basic content types defined in a standard Drupal 8 installation and how they can be used for a simple website.

Chapter 6, Structure, discusses how content can be structured once it has been created.

Chapter 7, Advanced Content, shows how to extend the basic concepts and create new content types, and why you might want to do this.

Chapter 8, Configuration, explains in detail each configuration option available in the standard Drupal 8 installation.

Chapter 9, Users and Access Control, shows how to control access to different areas of your Drupal site.

Chapter 10, Optional Features, presents various features of Drupal switched off in the default installation. This chapter explains what they are and what they do.

Chapter 11, Reports, shows the reports available in the standard installation and how you can use the data presented in it.

Chapter 12, Extending Drupal, discusses the modular nature of Drupal and how you can extend it to add more functionality.

Chapter 13, Theming Drupal, gives an introduction to theming a Drupal site.

Chapter 14, Getting Support, shows how the Open Source Drupal Community works now that we have reached the end of the instructional part of the book. However Drupal 8 is an extensive software framework and you should not expect to find all of the answers in a "Learning" book. In this chapter we discuss how the Open Source Drupal Community works and how you can engage with the community to get help and support for your Drupal project.

What you need for this book

In order to follow along with this book you will need to install Drupal on your own development environment. The steps to do this are given in *Chapter 2, Installation*. A laptop or desktop machine should be sufficient, you will not need a commercial web server to complete the exercises detailed in the chapters to follow. Drupal works in any modern browser. You will not need to edit any PHP code to complete the chapters in this book.

Who this book is for

If you want to learn Drupal 8 for the first time, or you are transitioning over from a previous version of Drupal, this is the book for you. The knowledge of PHP, MySQL, or HTML is not required.

Conventions

In this book, you will find a number of text styles that distinguish between different kinds of information. Here are some examples of these styles and an explanation of their meaning.

Code words in text, database table names, folder names, filenames, file extensions, pathnames, dummy URLs, user input, and Twitter handles are shown as follows: "The site-specific settings file is called `settings.php` and can be found in the `default` folder."

New terms and **important words** are shown in bold. Words that you see on the screen, for example, in menus or dialog boxes, appear in the text like this: "Select the language you want to install and click on **Save and continue**."

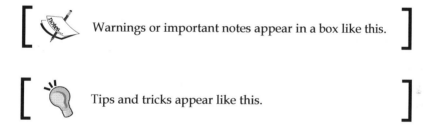

> Warnings or important notes appear in a box like this.

> Tips and tricks appear like this.

Reader feedback

Feedback from our readers is always welcome. Let us know what you think about this book—what you liked or disliked. Reader feedback is important for us as it helps us develop titles that you will really get the most out of.

To send us general feedback, simply e-mail feedback@packtpub.com, and mention the book's title in the subject of your message.

If there is a topic that you have expertise in and you are interested in either writing or contributing to a book, see our author guide at www.packtpub.com/authors.

Customer support

Now that you are the proud owner of a Packt book, we have a number of things to help you to get the most from your purchase.

Downloading the color images of this book

We also provide you with a PDF file that has color images of the screenshots/diagrams used in this book. The color images will help you better understand the changes in the output. You can download this file from http://www.packtpub.com/sites/default/files/downloads/Learning_Drupal_8_ColoredImages.pdf.

Errata

Although we have taken every care to ensure the accuracy of our content, mistakes do happen. If you find a mistake in one of our books—maybe a mistake in the text or the code—we would be grateful if you could report this to us. By doing so, you can save other readers from frustration and help us improve subsequent versions of this book. If you find any errata, please report them by visiting http://www.packtpub.com/submit-errata, selecting your book, clicking on the **Errata Submission Form** link, and entering the details of your errata. Once your errata are verified, your submission will be accepted and the errata will be uploaded to our website or added to any list of existing errata under the Errata section of that title.

To view the previously submitted errata, go to https://www.packtpub.com/books/content/support and enter the name of the book in the search field. The required information will appear under the **Errata** section.

Piracy

Piracy of copyrighted material on the Internet is an ongoing problem across all media. At Packt, we take the protection of our copyright and licenses very seriously. If you come across any illegal copies of our works in any form on the Internet, please provide us with the location address or website name immediately so that we can pursue a remedy.

Please contact us at copyright@packtpub.com with a link to the suspected pirated material.

We appreciate your help in protecting our authors and our ability to bring you valuable content.

eBooks, discount offers, and more

Did you know that Packt offers eBook versions of every book published, with PDF and ePub files available? You can upgrade to the eBook version at www.PacktPub.com and as a print book customer, you are entitled to a discount on the eBook copy. Get in touch with us at customercare@packtpub.com for more details.

At www.PacktPub.com, you can also read a collection of free technical articles, sign up for a range of free newsletters, and receive exclusive discounts and offers on Packt books and eBooks.

Questions

If you have a problem with any aspect of this book, you can contact us at questions@packtpub.com, and we will do our best to address the problem.

1
Introduction

What is Drupal?

Back in the old days (pre-1995ish), we used to have to download special software to our computers in order to buy things, look up things, and build things.

"Madness", I hear you say.

Of course those days are long gone. Nowadays, we all simply expect to be able do everything we need using a web browser. To put it another way, we all expect everything presented to us in some form of "web technology". But, what does it really mean in simple terms?

You probably already know that all the web pages that are a part of our everyday lives are written in the language of **HTML—Hyper Text Markup Language**.

If you've ever dug a little deeper, you might also know that the styling of web pages—the colors, typography, layout, and so on are controlled by **CSS—Cascading Style Sheets**.

Add some **JavaScript** into the mix, and web pages become a bit more interactive with things popping up and dropping down all over the place to make the experience a bit richer.

So, there it is. As good today, as it's always been...

Traditionally, piecing this all together involved a pretty detailed understanding of each of the three parts—it was all a bit too technical for many; it meant becoming fluent in these new "languages"; it meant you had to be a "coder".

So, what is **Drupal**? Where does it fit into all this?

It can be difficult to put a label on what Drupal actually is, since it is many different things to different people. We could start talking about terms such as "PHP-based social publishing software" and "web application framework", but let's not get into all that.

All you really need to understand right now is that Drupal is your LEGO-like toolkit for piecing together HTML, CSS, and JavaScript to build great websites.

Drupal is a tool that equips anyone, regardless of their level of experience with web technologies, to build a state-of-the-art website. True to the founder's original vision of providing a website-building framework that can be used to spectacular ends without having to learn to code. You no longer need to know HTML, CSS, and JavaScript to create a real state-of-the-art website. Now, that sounds good.

Having set the scene, let's go back in time and discover how we got to Drupal 8.

Dynamic web pages – a brief history

We used to piece together our web pages using HTML tags and styles all mixed together with JavaScript, images, and other file assets such as PDFs, Flash animations, and finally, the content itself.

The design, functionality, and the actual content were all mixed together to create the pages. These pages were also "static", in the sense that they could never change. The only way to update the actual content of the pages and/or their layout, cosmetic style, and fancy interactive moving parts was to be a "coder" and do some technical editing. Nasty!

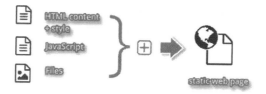

Originally proposed in 1994, it wasn't until the early 21st century (2001) that we managed to separate out web pages' style from their content with the introduction of CSS. Likewise, the fashion moved to splitting out the JavaScript code into separate, more manageable files too.

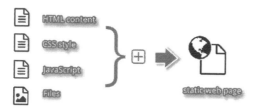

Even with this useful advance, the pages were still only static. What we were really seeking was a mechanism for having the actual content itself come from other dynamic sources and for the web pages to be generated on the fly. We needed to make our pages dynamic.

Enter the database

Then came a whole host of what we shall loosely refer to as code engines in various programming languages designed to achieve the dynamic approach: CGI, Perl, Python, PHP, Cold Fusion, ASP, JSP, Ruby, and numerous others.

Let's not worry about the technical differences between all these. What really matters here is that they all strived to meet the challenge of separating out the page structure, style, and content so that these elements could be organized in a more manageable fashion.

In all of the preceding approaches, instead of the content being embedded in the web page, it was now being stored in and retrieved from a database, and the HTML pages were being assembled on the fly from that data and a collection of site-themed elements. See the following for an illustration.

This means that our pages can rebuild themselves in response to users' input; communication became two-way between the users and the website. This was the birth of "Web 2.0".

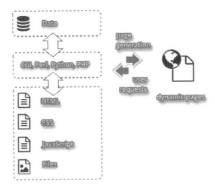

Drupal employs one of the aforementioned languages, namely PHP, to build data-driven pages and so provide us with a neat, manageable split between content, configuration, user accounts, and media assets such as images, documents, and video.

PHP is a very widely used open source scripting language that is especially suited to web development because it can be embedded into HTML pages. PHP "pages" are essentially HTML pages with embedded programming code that reshapes the contents of the HTML page dynamically before you get to see it in your browser.

The PHP code is executed on the server, and it generates a complete HTML page, which is then sent to your browser. As far as you are concerned, the end result is a fully formed HTML page, and you have no evidence that it was constructed dynamically by PHP.

Drupal is the clever PHP that brings together the various assets to form the actual visible pages, which are then made available to us across the web using a web server.

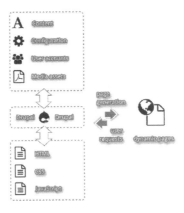

Drupal is completely free and always will be. It is open source. It is a software that is not owned by anyone but is instead developed collectively by a community of people interested in continually improving it as a platform.

Let's dwell a moment on the term "open source" so as to be clear about what it really means.

The word "source" here refers to the actual original program code written by the author. Programmers who have access to a computer program's source code can improve the program by adding features to it or fixing parts that don't always work correctly. The open source license actively promotes collaboration and sharing. Anyone can make modifications to source code and incorporate these changes into their own projects. Thus, open source projects benefit from a potentially infinite number of "authors". However good we might think we are at developing software, the community is better!

The *open source* label itself was created at a strategy meeting held in early 1998 in Palo Alto, California.

A worldwide community

It is important to understand that Drupal really is more than just the actual software. It is also a worldwide community of developers, designers, project managers, business innovators, technology specialists, and user-experience professionals. Community members all pull together to continually make Drupal ever more flexible, extensible, and standard compliant, so as to take advantage of emerging technologies. For a long time, the unofficial strapline of Drupal has been "come for the software, stay for the community," and this is certainly true in our experience.

The success of Drupal

So why does Drupal prosper and why is it steadily gaining momentum as the platform of choice for organizations large and small the world over? This question is answered in the following sections.

Multiple systems integration

We've become used to a diet of multiple software platforms and technologies each with its own cost, interface, storage, and security issues. You may be all too familiar with statements, such as:

"We have multiple systems working here, only some of which seem to talk to each other"

"You want a blog? Use WordPress for that".

Attempting to integrate a range of technologies is usually an expensive and never-ending business, and the management of the middleware (yet more layers of software) required to glue them together is a sizeable debt to be repaid, often over and over.

 With Drupal, you will find that you can do it all in one place and in a consistent, coordinated fashion.

Technical debt

"I had to start from scratch"

Anyone in the IT project business knows all too well that the underlying code can quickly become the reserve of the individual developer who actually wrote it. Often it is only when the particular individual leaves the company that the technical debt is realized. The developer may not have documented their approach, let alone the actual code that someone else inevitably has to take on. The legacy may contain all manner of unjustified assumptions, poor coding practices, "hidden features" (that is, bugs), and quick but irreversible fixes that close the doors to integration and further extension. All too often, in trying to deal with their inheritance, the new developer ends up re-inventing it all over again often with a new set of assumptions and with a potential new set of bugs.

With Drupal, you can at least be assured that the code has gone through a clearly defined community peer-review process, and opting to use the Drupal framework as the basis for building your solutions will go a long way to addressing concerns about the code quality and therefore technical debt.

Developer knowledge

"We can't seem to find quality Drupal developers"

However, we should not be naïve and pretend to ourselves that Drupal is the silver bullet we've all been waiting for. It comes with its own significant technical debt not least of which is the absolute necessity for having proper Drupal-savvy developers on your team. Drupal code is very framework specific, so one should not expect a competent PHP developer to be able to be truly effective with Drupal without an investment of time learning to understand how to properly work with the framework.

Drupal 8 initiatives to stay relevant such as its use of the PHP framework known as Symfony 2 — essentially a collection of well-respected state-of-the-art PHP components — have gone a long way to make the underlying code more familiar to modern PHP developers who are used to working with modern object-oriented PHP. However, investment in learning the Drupal way is still crucial.

With its growing library of free extension modules, themes (pre-built skins), and sizable developer community, Drupal is still probably the wisest choice and the most future-proof content management framework around.

 If you are considering adopting Drupal as your platform, then we strongly advise you to make certain that your developer team is professionally trained.

Modularity

Think of Drupal as a gigantic LEGO construction kit for would-be site builders. Drupal site builders develop websites by piecing together Drupal modules. Each module is designed to solve a particular problem but in a Drupal-compliant way, so as to keep all the doors open to integrating with the enormous repository of other community-written modules that are out there.

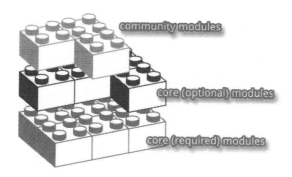

There's a module for that

When we plan to add a new feature to our website, the first step is to look around and see what's already been done by community members to see if "there's a module for that". For example, imagine that you want to create a community site where members can:

1. Login in and post-up articles and invite other members' comments.
2. Share posts with a variety of common social networking sites such as Twitter, Facebook, and the like.
3. Automate actions such as redirecting some users to key pages on log in.
4. Optionally promote their posts in animated highlighting carousels.

This can be done by simply performing the following steps:

1. A straight out of the box—a freshly installed—Drupal site will enable posting and commenting using only the core modules.
2. This is provided by *Easy Social* module—at the time of writing, v8.x-3.0-alpha3 (`drupal.org/project/easy_social`).
3. This is provided by the *Rules* module—at the time of writing, v8.x-3.x-unstable4 (`drupal.org/project/rules`).
4. This is probably best provided by *Nivo Slider* module—at the time of writing, v 8.x-1.4 (`drupal.org/project/nivo_slider`).

For pretty much anything you might want to add to your website, there's a very high chance that among the many modules out there, the very thing you are after has already been coded and posted up into the Drupal community site for public consumption at:

`www.drupal.org`.

While it is still early days with regard to many of the most commonly used community modules being ready as stable Drupal 8 releases, the number is growing every day.

Some Drupal history

It all started in 1999 when the founder, Dries Buytaert, began working on a simple website that incorporated a message board software application while he was an undergraduate at the University of Antwerp. For the next 2 years, he and a small group of friends used and developed the as yet unnamed application. In January 2001, they named their creation Drupal, open sourced it, and started the `Drupal.org` community site.

The rest, as they say, is history. The community continues to grow at an ever-increasing rate and the attendance figures at the official **Drupalcon** conferences worldwide are testament to the developer community's interest.

Language choice

Drupal is written in the open source scripting language PHP.

Because of PHP's relative simplicity and its rather forgiving nature, it's the perfect language choice for the newcomer because it can be learned fairly quickly and can be "assimilated" gradually by dissecting existing Drupal modules. This is certainly true at least for the Drupal 7 core. Drupal 8 code being object oriented, on the other hand, is a somewhat different story because object orientation is a concept that can be initially difficult to grasp for those without prior training.

Is Drupal a framework or platform?

Drupal is not, as is commonly quoted, just a **content management system (CMS)**. It's actually much more than that and we use the terms "framework" and "platform" quite deliberately in the opening paragraph to ignite the debate as to quite which of these Drupal is.

Once you've got to grips with the Drupal approach, you'll find that you can quickly and easily configure it as a content-management system. However, given its versatile and highly-bendable nature, you can in fact use it to build anything from a simple brochure-ware site to a fully-fledged web application with a huge community membership and which interfaces with a myriad enterprise services: Facebook, Twitter, Google, YouTube, Flickr, and whatever else is around the next corner.

The question still remains the same; is Drupal a framework—something with which we can build things, or is it a platform—something from which we launch other web products?

Let's say that we use Drupal to build a website that we intend to re-use over and over again as the basis for a collection of other sites. In this respect, what we have built is indeed a platform in its own right; a platform from which we can spawn all those other sites.

Let's say that we use Drupal to build a web application that integrates with a whole range of services in the wider world, again we have built a platform.

In both of the preceding examples, we created platforms, but in both cases, they are built on the Drupal framework.

Embracing other communities' frameworks

Drupal 8 is also a framework that openly embraces other open source frameworks: Symfony 2 (PHP), jQuery, Backbone, Modernizr, and Underscore (JavaScript) to name a few. The Drupal community does not seek to reinvent the wheel, but rather to integrate and build upon others' efforts and achievements.

How an open source community works

Software development based on the sharing and collaborative improvement of source code has a long history. In the late '90s, interest and participation in collaborative working increased markedly with two initiatives: the mainstream recognition of the Linux operating system and the release of the Netscape browser's source code.

Drupal likes to think of itself as a meritocracy, that is, those who are most influential in the community are those providing the best input, be it code, user experience, documentation, or otherwise. Neither individuals nor businesses can buy influence in the community, although they can of course achieve this by paying their staff to work on specific areas of interest.

The majority of people contributing to Drupal are doing so voluntarily in their own time. Some are sponsored by their employer, while some are just trying to solve a specific problem that interests them personally.

When contributing a new module to Drupal, the module's developer (also referred to as the **maintainer**) is entering into an informal agreement with the community that they will continue to maintain and update the module.

The mindset of the community is always to give back.

Those new to open source often struggle with this concept. There is a strange conflict that says "I don't want to give away my work"—when in fact your work is itself based on the unpaid efforts of thousands of others.

An appreciation of others' efforts is also key to the Drupal community. The Drupal issue queues are the place where bugs and feature requests are placed for both core and contributed modules. When reporting bugs, other community members are generally grateful for the efforts of the maintainer and offer constructive feedback or fixes.

People seem to understand that when you are not paying for something you don't have the right to be rude or disrespectful—although it's fair to say this should never be an option. That said, there can be heated discussions from time to time on contentious issues.

Summary

In summary, Drupal is what you make of it. You can simply download and build a site with Drupal 8 using just the core functionality, or you can extend the functionality using modules freely available in the community. Going further, you can develop your own modules and themes and make Drupal 8 the base for a complex e-commerce delivery system, if that's what you want to do. Like the LEGO analogy, the limitation is only your imagination and, maybe to some extent, your individual coding skills.

The remaining chapters in this book will take you step by step through the modules and functionality you get with a stock Drupal 8 installation without any community-contributed modules. This will show just how much you can already achieve before you have to think about extending Drupal, let alone coding.

2
Installation

This chapter takes you through the steps for installing **Drupal 8** using a local development environment. At the time of writing, the most up-to-date version of Drupal 8 is the 8.01 release, which can be downloaded from:

`https://www.drupal.org/project/drupal`

System requirements

Drupal 8 is a **PHP**-based software application and as such requires the following:

PHP

The following PHP version is required for the installation of Drupal 8:

- PHP 5.5.9 or higher

Web server options

One of the following:

- Apache
- Nginx
- Microsoft IIS

Database options

One of the following:

- MySQL 5.5.3 or above with PDO
- PostgreSQL 3.6.8 or above with PDO
- SQLite 3.6.8 or above
- MariaDB 5.5.20 (or greater)
- Percona Server 5.2.8 (or greater)

Browser options

One of the following:

- Internet Explorer 9.x and above
- Firefox 5.x and above
- Opera 12 and above
- Safari 5.x and above
- Google Chrome

Up-to-date system requirements can be found at `https://drupal.org/requirements`.

Setting up a development environment

When you are getting started with Drupal, you may not have access to a web server in order to install it.

Often it is much easier at first to work on your own computer rather than have to worry about setting up an internet-hosted server environment by setting up a local stack of Apache, MySQL, PHP, which are often referred to generically as **AMP** stacks and as **LAMP**, **WAMP**, or **MAMP** stacks on Linux, Windows, or Mac, respectively.

Full instructions for installing Drupal manually into local stack can be found at: `https://www.drupal.org/documentation/install` but if you are not super confident at installing things like this manually, we recommend that you go for the Acquia Dev desktop method described below.

Free cloud hosting

Acquia is a company founded by the creator of Drupal, Dries Buytaert, which specializes in Drupal. **Pantheon** is another company which specializes in Drupal. Both of these offer a free sandbox hosting for Drupal.

`https://www.acquia.com/free` and `https://www.getpantheon.com` are cloud offerings which allow you to host and develop a Drupal 8 site on a hosted Internet-based web server. Both services offer a one-click install of Drupal. If you choose to use one of these, you can skip directly now to the section entitled *Installing Drupal 8*.

Acquia Dev Desktop

Acquia offers a free local development environment for Windows and Mac called **Acquia Dev Desktop** that you can download and install on your own local machine in order to run Drupal 8 in the shortest possible time.

Download either the Windows or Mac version of the Acquia Dev Desktop from `https://www.acquia.com/downloads` and install it selecting the defaults for the various settings.

Once you have completed the installation, you will be offered the opportunity to run it.

When you do, you will see the stack start up in the background, and in the foreground you will see a welcome window offering some choices.

The first option is what we are after right now, so click on it:

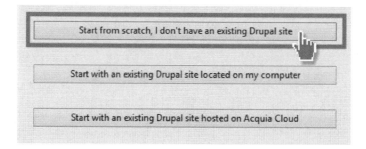

If for any reason you cannot access the preceding pop-up choice window, you can always get back there by clicking on the **+** sign in the bottom left-hand corner with choices including **New Drupal site...** that you should select:

At the time of going to click on it, there are several choices available to you, some notable ones being:

- **Drupal**: This is the official Drupal 7 core. No extras added.
- **Drupal 8**: This is the official Drupal 8 core. These official releases come bundled with a variety of modules and themes to give you a good starting point to help build your site.

Also included are a number of other distributions—various ready-to-go packages built around Drupal 7, most notably the following:

- **Drupal Commons**: This lets you create content-rich community websites built on Drupal 7. You can easily add wikis, calendars, groups, and other social web capabilities.
- **OpenAtrium**: This is an intranet in a box' that has group spaces to allow different teams to have their own conversations and collaboration.
- **OpenPublic**: This is designed for open government requirements, such as improving citizen services, providing public access to data and a public forum for two-way communication with agencies, without compromising accessibility, security, or usability.
- **OpenScholar**: This helps the management of educational institutions by providing Drupal-based professor pages, class catalogs, sandboxes, and extra tools for administration.

Locate the Drupal 8 offering and select install to begin the installation process:

Optionally, in the following dialog and in order to keep your installation precisely in line with the given screenshots, change the following:

1. Local codebase folder.
2. Local site name to Drupal 8 as shown in the following:

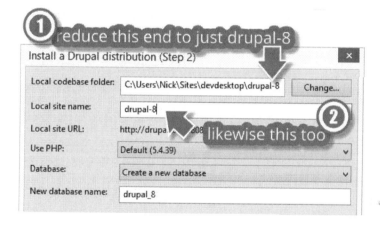

Now, select **Finish**. Since you are setting up Drupal from scratch and have no pre-existing database, all the remaining default options will be fine, and a database named `drupal_8` will be created automatically. Apache will be appropriately configured, as will your local host file.

> **Dev Desktop** sets up Apache on port 8083 rather than the standard (default) port of 80 so that it can be run on a local system without administrator privileges and without interfering with other local services. This means that when talking to sites governed by the Dev Desktop, you should always suffix your URLs with `:8083`.

Installing Drupal 8

Now that you have your server environment configured, whether it be a cloud sandbox, your own web server, or the Dev Desktop, the steps to install Drupal 8 are the same, only the URL will be different. In the case of the Dev Desktop, go to `http://drupal-8.dd:8083/install.php` in your web browser.

 Note that the Dev Desktop adds on the '.dd' suffix to the domain.

The Dev Desktop makes launching your new site very easy because it provides a shortcut link from within the control panel window:

You will see a number of option screens during the installation process, each of which we will walk through now.

Select the language you want to install and click on **Save and continue**. This is the language the user interface will be presented in:

Next, you will be asked which of two built-in installation profiles you wish to use.

Note that if are using the Dev Desktop then the Standard profile will be chosen automatically and so the whole step will be omitted.

If you have installed manually or you are on one of the cloud offerings, opt for the Standard one for this tutorial then click Save and continue.

Next, you will need your database login details.

If you are using the Acquia Dev Desktop to develop your site locally, then you can just leave the defaults as follows, because it creates the database and user itself (you do not need to, and should not, set a database password). Please note that on any hosted environment you would of course always add a secure password.

If you are using your own web server or an alternative local AMP stack, you will need to complete the appropriate database credentials for a database that you have already set up in advance:

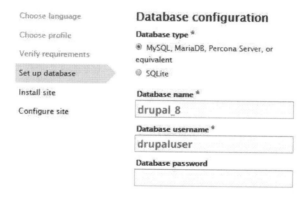

Select **Save and continue**. Next, you will see a progress screen entitled **Installing Drupal**, which details the progress of installing each of the standard core modules that are active in a base install:

This may take a few minutes, depending on the speed of your local machine.

Configuring your Drupal 8 site

Once all the modules have been installed and the progress reaches 100%, you will be presented with the **Configure site** dialog as shown here:

This step contains quite a few fields, so the different sections have been broken up into individual screenshots.

The value you enter in the **Site name** field will be used in the header of the site (depending on your theme settings) and also in the browser title bar. For now, leave it set to *drupal-8*.

Note that we changed the site name down from My site to simply Drupal 8 purely for neatness:

The e-mail address entered is the main contact address of the site and will be used as the sender address by default whenever an e-mail is sent out by the site. The site maintenance account that is automatically created, now is the master account for the Drupal site—often referred to as the admin, user, user 1, or uid:1. This account has special privileges and is not subject to any kind of permission-based controls.

Due to the extremely high powered nature of this user, it is especially important in any real site to use a strong password rather then something like `admin`, as we are using in this tutorial.

The e-mail address will be copied from the site e-mail address by default, but it does not have to be the same.

For security in a real-life Drupal site, it is strongly recommended you use a non-standard username for the site maintenance account (and not something common or easily guessable).

However, for the sake of simplicity, we will just use `admin` for the username and `admin` for the password.

Next, you can set the default country and time zone for your site. The values chosen here will affect the various other regional settings in the site—for example, date formats:

REGIONAL SETTINGS

Default country

| United Kingdom | ▼ |

Select the default country for the site.

Default time zone

| Europe / London | ▼ |

The final installation step asks if you would like to check for updates automatically. It is highly recommended that you leave this switched on as you will then be notified when there are new versions of Drupal core or any contributed modules you have added.

If you do not select **Receive email notifications**, you will be notified of available updates via a notice on screen when you are logged onto the site with the site maintenance account active (as indeed you are now):

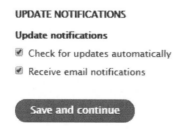

UPDATE NOTIFICATIONS

Update notifications

☑ Check for updates automatically

☑ Receive email notifications

Save and continue

Select **Save and continue**.

Your installation of Drupal 8 is now complete, and you will see a message that says **Congratulations, you installed Drupal!**

You will also see the "Toolbar" module providing access to: **Manage**, **Shortcuts**, and your (**admin**) account page, and beneath that, the "Tray" as shown in the following screenshot:

Congratulations, your Drupal site is installed and ready to go!

Troubleshooting your installation

If your site does not install correctly, there are some configuration tips that you might want to check.

 Note that if you are using the Dev Desktop, you need not do any of this.

Memory settings

Sometimes, memory settings may need to be adjusted to get your site running correctly. Here are some suggestions on things to adjust.

If you are getting out of memory errors during installation, you can try increasing the memory available to Drupal.

When you imported the Drupal 8 site, the Dev Desktop will have created a site folder, which contains a settings file specifically. The site-specific settings file is called `settings.php` and can be found in the `default` folder.

Note that the `default` folder is also linked to the `drupal-8.dd` symlink.

Locate and edit the file:

```
/sites/default/settings.php
```

Add a new line:

```
ini_set('memory_limit', '128M');
```

This increases the memory allocated to PHP when running your site. `128M` should be sufficient, but if you still have problems, try increasing this. Note that by default, the file should have been set to read only on your system and therefore you may need to take some action before you can save your changes.

PHP timeouts

If you have a slower computer, sometimes the PHP timeout settings needs to be increased to allow more time for the installation steps to be completed.

In the same settings file as before:

```
docroot/sites/default/settings.php
```

Add a new line:

```
ini_set('max_execution_time', '240');
```

The `240` here refers to the number of seconds and this should be sufficient, but if you still have problems, try increasing this again.

Trusted host patterns

If you visit the page `/admin/reports/status` then you will see a warning informing you that **Trusted Host Settings** are not enabled.

Drupal 8 use a trusted host mechanism, where site administrators can whitelist hostnames. The mechanism now can be configured in the `settings.php` file.

Setting the pattern as show here will inform Drupal that all sites hosted locally using the Dev Desktop – this with a URL ending in '.dd' - are trusted.

```
$settings['trusted_host_patterns'] = array(
  '^.*\.dd$',
);
```

Summary

By following the steps in this chapter, you should now have a full clean install of the Drupal 8. Next, we will look at fundamental Drupal concepts and the terminology that you will come across while learning to build your first Drupal 8 site.

3
Basic Concepts

When you first start learning Drupal, there are some key terms that you will come across, which are used to define the components of the system. These are:

- Modules
- Entities
- Nodes
- Fields
- Taxonomy
- Blocks
- Views

Understanding these terms and how they relate to one another will ease your journey into Drupal. Using the correct terminology when reporting issues will mean you are more likely to be understood by the community and therefore are more likely to get help as and when you need it.

In this chapter, we will look at each of the components to provide a better foundation for learning Drupal.

Modules

As we discussed in *Chapter 1, Introduction*, Drupal is highly modular in its design; you can switch on or off various bits of functionality by enabling/disabling modules, and you can also extend the system by adding new ones.

Other systems may describe modules as **plugins**—the two are synonymous.

Core and contrib modules

The term Drupal core refers to the set of modules that are present in the main Drupal download that you have just installed. You can achieve a great deal using just these, but developers around the world have created their own modules for specific areas of functionality, which you can also use free of charge.

Collectively, these community-contributed modules are referred to as **contrib** modules.

All modules can be downloaded from the Drupal website (`https://www.drupal.org`), and each one has its own individual project page. The project page for each module contains the downloadable code, releases, documentation, and links to the issue queue that we will discuss later in this chapter.

Where the core modules live

In Drupal 8, the core modules are located in the `/core/modules` folder.

 Prior to Drupal 8, core modules were located in the `/modules` folder.

Where your extension modules should live

You should never put your own modules or any contributed modules in the `core` folder.

It is recommended that you place your downloaded and custom module extensions in the `/modules` folder located in the Drupal root.

Following this rule will allow you to apply upgrades to the Drupal core system.

 The `/sites/all/modules` structure, which was recommended in previous versions of Drupal, is still supported, but should not be used by default.

You can structure your modules folder however you like, but the standard convention is to have a structure in which you clearly segregate community (contrib) modules from any custom modules that you may have written yourself.

Thus, from the top level, the module folder structure is:

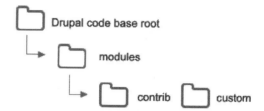

An example community module

As an example, let's look at a typical community module, in this case, the Google Analytics module. The Google Analytics module enables you to track visitors to your site using the popular Google Analytics service and can be found at:

```
https://www.drupal.org/project/google_analytics
```

The project page will contain a description of the module and one or more links to download it. Modules may be available to support multiple versions of Drupal. You should be downloading modules marked as version 8.x.

The following screenshot shows a typical module project page, in this case, the Google Analytics module:

Evaluating new modules

You should try to evaluate modules from the perspective of the requirements of the site you are building before you go ahead and download them. There are thousands of modules out there in the community; some are great, some are good, and some don't have a lot of traction, so be sure to choose the ones that are right for your use case.

Before you start downloading modules, first consider the following:

- How many downloads does the module have?

  The more popular a module is, the more the code will have been analyzed and bugs reported.

- How many installs does the module have?

  This is only a guideline as not all sites report back their usage.

Project Information

Maintenance status: Actively maintained
Development status: Under active development

Module categories: Statistics , Third-party Integration

Reported installs: **394,197** sites currently report using this module. statistics.
Downloads: 3,039,566
Last modified: October 1, 2015

- Who is the maintainer?

  Some maintainers have many modules which they look after. Maintainer reputation is also an indicator of quality: Is the module in active development? How responsive is the maintainer to the issue queue? When was the most recently committed update? and so on.

- Open bugs and issues?

  Every module has its own issue queue (discussed in *Chapter 14, Getting Support*). The bug count should not necessarily scare you off. Popular modules have plenty of people reporting bugs; some may not be bugs at all, and some will be duplicates or support requests.

Maintainers for Google
Analytics

hass - 1141 commits
last: 2 weeks ago, first: 8 years ago

budda - 50 commits
last: 3 years ago, first: 9 years ago

View all committers
View commits

Documentation

Some modules have it, while some rely on a README file. You can see all of this information in the bar on the right-hand side of the module page.

Module versions

Some modules will have a -dev version listed. This is the most up-to-date code, but may be unstable. Running a -dev module on a production site is *not* recommended; although pragmatically speaking, since Drupal 8 has only recently been released, it may well be something that you are forced to do. Most modules will have a recommended version that is currently supported by the maintainer. If in doubt, always use the recommended version.

Downloads

Recommended releases

Version	Download	Date
8.x-2.0-rc1	tar.gz (40.67 KB)	zip (59.39 KB)	2015-Nov-22
7.x-2.1	tar.gz (38.72 KB)	zip (45.83 KB)	2014-Nov-29
6.x-4.1	tar.gz (37.5 KB)	zip (43.08 KB)	2014-Nov-29

Development releases

Version	Download	Date
8.x-2.x-dev	tar.gz (40.91 KB)	zip (59.88 KB)	2015-Nov-29
7.x-2.x-dev	tar.gz (39.07 KB)	zip (46.29 KB)	2015-Nov-15
6.x-4.x-dev	tar.gz (37.87 KB)	zip (43.6 KB)	2015-Nov-04

Entities, nodes, and fields

When working with Drupal, one of the most important concepts to understand is that you are not just building pages, you are building page containers that consist of components. These components are made up of things called *entities*.

Entities

Everything you create in Drupal is referred to as an **entity**.

Nodes

Most viewable content you create will be of a particular type of entity known as a **node entity**.

Node types

You may often hear the terms "node entity", "node type", and "content type" interchanged routinely, so it's a good idea to think of these terms as synonymous.

There can be many different types of node entities in any given site, but in the standard installation, there are only two content types (node types) defined and they are: **Basic page** and **Article**.

Fields

All node entities contain a **Title** property and one or more fields, an example of which is the **Body** field. When creating an Article node, we see the following properties, fields, and their types exposed to us ready to populate:

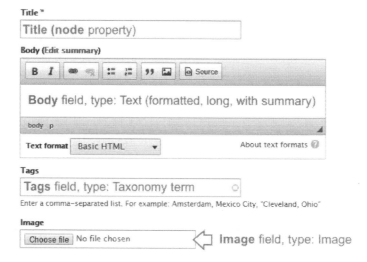

Adding new fields

One of the most useful things about Drupal is the ease with which you can add new fields to existing content types. You might, for example, wish to add a date to an article if that article relates to an event. This can be done in literally moments as you will see shortly.

Field types

In the standard profile we installed earlier, the available field types are as follows:

General

Boolean	A yes or no field or checkbox.
Comments	Allow visitors to the site to add comments.
Date	A date and time.

Number

List (float or integer)	A predefined list of values that the user can pick from when creating new content.
Number (decimal, float, or integer)	To hold a number in a specified format.

Reference

Content	A preconfigured reference field for setting up a relationship between one entity and another. Defaults to the node entity type.
File	A preconfigured reference field for setting up a relationship between one entity and binary file entity, such as a PDF.
Image	A preconfigured reference field, similar to a File field, but intended for images that will be displayed visually.
Taxonomy term	A preconfigured reference field to useful for creating an association with one or more taxonomy (classification) terms and a specified Taxonomy vocabulary.
User	A preconfigured reference field for setting up a relationship to one or User entities.
Other	A reference field useful for referencing any type of other entity, for example, Commerce Product(s).

Text

Text (formatted, long)	For use where there will be longer descriptive text possibly with html markup.
Text (formatted, long, with summary)	As for Text (formatted, long) but with an additional short version of the text that can be used in a teaser for good SEO.
Text	For short text, generally fewer than 256 characters without markup.

As we saw earlier, the Article content type that is defined by the standard install profile without any additional configuration contains the following fields:

- Body: Text (formatted, long, with summary)
- Comment: (Comments)
- Image: (Image)
- Tags: (Taxonomy term)

LABEL	MACHINE NAME	FIELD TYPE	OPERATIONS
Body	body	Text (formatted, long, with summary)	Edit ▾
Comments	comment	Comments	Edit ▾
Image	field_image	Image	Edit ▾
Tags	field_tags	Taxonomy term	Edit ▾

You can customize any content type, delete any of the existing fields, or add new ones to suit your design. For example, if we want to create a field that allows us to add PDF files as attachments to Articles, we would simply add a new **Reference | File** type field.

This has been no more than a brief glance at some isolated screenshots for now, because the topic of field editing will be discussed in detail in *Chapter 7, Advanced Content*.

Field settings

Fields can be set to have a single value, a fixed maximum number of values, or an unlimited number of values. For example, we can set the Article content type to allow a single PDF file to be uploaded, or we can set up the field to accept any number of file attachments.

Field widgets

Widgets provide configuration options for how the field is presented to the user when creating and editing content. For example, a Text (long) field may be presented with a **WYSIWYG (What You See Is What You Get)** editor window or as a simple plain text field. If, for example, we were using a Date-type field, then we might prefer to present the content editing team with a drop-down menu for each element: Day, Month, and Year in a standard format such as yyyy/mm/dd in place of the default simple text entry of a date.

Form display

Whenever you are editing an item of content through the Drupal user interface (UI), we refer to the UI as the "Edit form". Without any doubt, you will want to arrange the edit form with the fields in the best possible order to help your content editors, so Drupal allows a high degree of control over this for, via the following:

Managing the form display

Strictly speaking, the Title is not a field, it is a property of the node entity but along with all the other fields it is still configurable here:

Managing field display

Similarly, all the fields rendered in the final content view have display-related settings too. In the example below we are looking at the settings for the Image field:

Drupal 8 core entity types

We established earlier that all of the actual items of "content" on a Drupal site (Articles, pages, and so on) are collectively referred to as **nodes**. Put another way, they are Node entities.

Others types of entity in the standard Drupal installation are: Comment, Custom block, Taxonomy term, and User.

Each of these other four entity types has its own set of specialized properties and fields. For example, the User entity, unlike the node entity, does not have the "published" property, but it does have a property relating to user registration settings. Similarly, it also has a specialized field entitled Picture for holding the user's image.

You can extend existing entities by adding more fields any time you like.

You can also define completely new entity types. For example, the Drupal commerce solution provided by the Commerce suite of modules defines, among others, entities to represent Products and Orders. These custom commerce entity types have properties and fields, which are custom-built precisely for selling online; Product entities, for example, have a SKU property and an intelligent Price field.

This approach allows you to create a structured data model to suit the needs of your particular website.

Taxonomy

One of the most powerful features of Drupal is the taxonomy system.

The word **taxonomy** comes from the ancient Greek word meaning 'the practice and science of the classification of things.

Consider a real-world example where Drupal might be used to manage, search, and display your music collection. It would be very useful to be able to categorize tracks within, for example, genre, because that way you could easily filter the entire collection down to say "soul" or "disco". Moreover, if you categorize the music tempo to say "slow", "medium", and "upbeat", then preparing a playlist of slow soul tracks would be simple just as you probably routinely do when using a dedicated organizer such as iTunes.

Thus, Drupal's taxonomy system is simply a means of enabling you to classify your content in many different ways.

The core taxonomy system allows you to define one or more vocabularies, each of which is a list of terms. For example, you may want to define an Article category vocabulary and associate it with your Article content type. The Article category vocabulary could contain terms such as "blog" and "news", thus enabling you to classify your Articles. The articles classified as blog appear on the blog page, and those categorized as news appearing on the news page.

A more abstract example might be to use taxonomy to categorize things by color. The vocabulary might be entitled `Color` and then you would have the actual colors as the terms.

You could then use the `Color` taxonomy to classify products such as t-shirts, socks, footballs, and so on, on a commerce site.

Fixed terms versus or tags

Taxonomies can be structured to have a fixed set of terms as discussed earlier, or they can be *tag based* in that the terms are defined as required when the content is being created just as you do when you are tagging content on say Facebook.

The Standard installation already has a single tag-based vocabulary called **Tags** associated with the Article content type.

 Careful planning of your taxonomy is essential to the ease of use and management of your website.

Blocks

If you have a layout that contains sidebars, headers, or footers, you will most likely have content that is repeated between pages. If you edit this content in one place, you would expect it to be updated on every page.

This is where blocks come in.

In Drupal 8, there is another entity type called a **block**.

A block is a piece of content that can be placed in a specific region of a page, and you can set rules that determine when (on which actual pages) the block appears, depending on various conditions such as the page URL or the currently logged in user's role(s).

An example of a block is the `Main menu`.

A typical simple website page template will often have a header, footer, and perhaps, left and right sidebar regions as shown in the following diagram:

Header
Menu

Sidebar first	Content	Sidebar second

Footer

Within these page template regions, you can add repeating content such as the site logo, a menu, shopping cart, terms and conditions, or other items of content.

Because Drupal is a modular framework, modules can define a block that you can place on your site. For example, the `Commerce` module provides a "Shopping cart" block.

You can also create custom blocks, which are essentially individual blocks of hand-coded HTML.

The important point to remember here is that much of the content on your Drupal site appears one way or another, as a series of blocks and blocks are placed within regions on the page.

Views

Once you have started to create content, it won't be very long before you find yourself in a situation where you need to create lists of it, as follows:

- A list of article titles with each title linked to the article detail
- A list of article "teasers" (shortened versions) linked to the full detail
- A list of articles associated with a particular taxonomy term

The core module `Views` is a powerful module that enables you to do all this and much more.

Views is a powerful and flexible query-building and content-display tool that can be used to build complex content listing pages to present your content the way you want.

You can specify the number of items to display in a list and publish your view to a specific URL (a page) or as a block to be included on one or more pages.

There are a number of built-in views included in the standard profile, which we will explore later. For example, Drupal enables you to quickly and easily mark content to be "Promoted to the front page" and the following screenshot shows the default Drupal front-page View, which lists all that content:

Article no. 1

Submitted by admin on Tue, 15/12/2015 - 14:37

Ut wisi enim ad minim veniam, quis nostrud exerci tation ullamcorper suscipit lobortis nisl ut aliquip.

Article no. 2

Submitted by admin on Tue, 15/12/2015 - 14:40

Lorem ipsum dolor sit amet, consetetur sadipscing elitr, sed diam nonumy eirmod tempor invidunt ut labore et dolore magna aliquyam erat, sed diam voluptua.

The Views module has been a staple of the Drupal site builders' toolkit for many years, but Drupal 8 is the first version of Drupal to include Views in the core module set.

In short, Views is a flexible query-building and content-display tool that can be used to build and present complex sets of filtered content. Views is so popular that almost every Drupal site uses it in some form or another. For this reason, the decision was made to move it into the Drupal 8 core.

You will see how to create views in detail later in *Chapter 6, Structure*.

Users, roles, and permissions

In order to log in to your Drupal 8 site, you will need a user account.

A site maintenance account was created automatically when you installed Drupal, and the user can perform all actions on this site. You may hear this user referred to as user 1, which is a reference to the user ID in the database.

A user is another form of entity, and like all other entity types, this means that you can add fields to the user definition in order to include more information in the user account such as forename, surname, and telephone number.

Each user is assigned one or more roles, and roles have permissions attached to determine exactly what the user is permitted to do when logged into the site. Standard roles are:

- **Anonymous user**: Assigned to anyone not logged into the site—visitors
- **Authenticated user**: This is assigned to anyone logged in to the site
- **Administrator**: This is for site owners, site maintainers, and site builders

You can, and most likely will, create additional roles for use on your site.

Drupal modules can add their own set of permissions. There is a permissions page where you can view and configure permissions for each role. You will find this page by navigating to **Manage | People | Permissions**.

The following example is an excerpt of the permissions page showing the custom permissions defined by the Comment module.

PERMISSION	ANONYMOUS USER	AUTHENTICATED USER	ADMINISTRATOR
Skip comment approval	☐	✓	✓
View comments	✓	✓	✓

Each role is assigned any number of these permissions, and then each user is assigned any number of roles. This design allows you to create a very fine-grained permission system in your Drupal site.

We will be covering roles and permissions in detail in *Chapter 9, Users and Access Control*.

Themes

A Drupal **theme** is the engine that provides the framework for the visual layout and design of your site, including bringing together the CSS, JavaScript, images, and colors. A Drupal theme itself determines the visual design of the website you are building.

In the standard install, there are a number of basic themes provided, and you can switch between them at any time.

The Standard profile installation ships with the `Bartik` theme. This theme is comprised of 17 page regions into which you can place one or more blocks. The 17 regions are shown in the following diagram:

Secondary menu

Header

Primary menu

Highlighted

Featured top

Breadcrumb

Sidebar first	Content	Sidebar second

Featured bottom first	Featured bottom second	Featured bottom third

Footer first	Footer second	Footer third	Footer fourth

Footer fifth

As you can see from the preceding diagram, the list of default regions for the Bartik theme and their relative positions on the page is enough to fill the layout of many sites.

Page and theme template regions will be covered in detail in *Chapter 13, Theming Drupal*.

Just as with modules, you can download themes from `https://www.drupal.org/` or you can create your own.

All themes have a settings page allowing you to change certain elements of the display, for example the color scheme used or whether to display the site logo and name. More complex themes have a greater range of settings within them.

Administration themes

There are also themes that are designed for use when visiting administrative pages, such as when managing users or create actual content. Themes such as these are known as **administration themes** or **admin themes** for short.

Drupal 8 ships with `Seven` as its admin theme.

A lot of effort has been made in Drupal 8 to ensure that admin themes work well on mobile devices allowing you to edit your content while on the move.

Base themes and subthemes

Some themes are not designed as finished products, but instead as starting points for your own theme development. These are commonly referred to as **base themes**. You can, and should, extend and override a base theme by creating a **subtheme**.

Themes will be covered in more detail in *Chapter 13, Theming Drupal*.

Hooks

An important concept in Drupal is the concept of module **hooks**. A module can expose one or more hooks empowering other modules to modify its behavior.

This means that if a module doesn't do exactly what you want, you can use a hook to "hook into" the process and change that module's behavior without having to change the original module code. Moreover, it means that when the original module whose behavior you have overridden gets updates, you'll be able to reap the benefits of the update while still keeping your modification(s) in place.

An example is `hook_entity_update`—a hook that is called after anything (any entity) is saved. Other modules may want to perform an action of their own in response to an entity update, and so we will also implement this hook.

Implementing hooks in your own modules is beyond the scope of this getting started book, but it's important to understand the terminology that you will no doubt come across as you continue working with Drupal.

For much more detail about the available hooks in Drupal, visit `https://api.drupal.org`.

Summary

This chapter introduced some key terminology used within Drupal 8, so you will know how to describe your system and understand online documentation and issues. Before continuing be sure that you have understood each of the terms such as modules, entities, nodes, fields, taxonomy, blocks, and views.

In the next chapter, we will start to experiment with your new Drupal 8 installation and work through the different functionality provided by the `Standard` profile.

4
Getting Started with the UI

The Drupal 8 user interface

In this chapter, we will walk you through the key parts of the standard Drupal 8 **User Interface (UI)** UI focusing our attention on the main visible components like the **Toolbar**, **Shortcuts** and Drupal's main administrative menu, the Administration menu.

As you work through this chapter, please keep in mind that the intention here is merely to provide you with a quick overview and that much more detail and guided tutorial assignments will follow in later chapters.

Logging out

When you first visit your new Drupal 8 site immediately after installation at: `http://drupal-8.dd:8083` you will do so, from the point of view of the `admin` user, that is, you are logged in as the special user with user ID (`uid`) set to 1.

To see the site from an anonymous site visitor's perspective, click on the **Log out** link at the top right of the page:

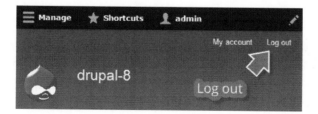

Logging in

You will now see only the login link at the top right corner of the page:

Log back in using the credentials you set up in *Chapter 2, Installation*.

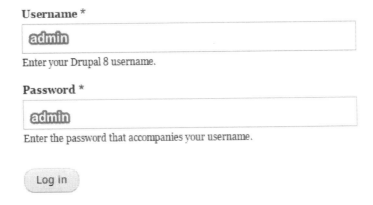

After logging in again, click on the **Home** tab or Drupal logo to go back to the front page.

Front page

We will now walk you through the page in order to illustrate what we were talking about back in *Chapter 3, Basic Concepts*, when we referred to pages being made up of **blocks** and **views**:

If your screen does not look exactly like the previous screenshot, try changing the width of your browser. The page layout will change, depending on the available size of the window. Matching the window size we used for the screenshots will help you get acquainted more quickly.

The default front page comprises the following elements:

1.   The **Toolbar,** which in turn contains four icons: **Manage**, **Shortcuts**, the currently logged in user (**admin**), and at the right-hand end, the **Edit** toggle icon that reveals / hides the contextual links (the encircled pencil icons that appear as you hover over editable content, see later).

2.   The **Tray**, which is immediately underneath the Toolbar, is a set of illustrated links that relates to the top level of the Administration menu.

3.   The **Main menu,** which is also hard coded in the default theme page template.

4.   The **Search block** is provided by the Search module, which is active by default.

5.   The **Main content (a view)** of the page in this case is provided by a View, which lists all of the content of any type that has been promoted to the front page. On a brand new site, there isn't any content, so don't expect to see much here.

6.   The **Tools menu**, like most things, exposed as a block.

In addition, at the bottom of the page you will see the Footer, which contains the following:

1. The **Footer menu (a block),** which again can be contributed to by any module. In a fresh installation, the only module which is contributing a menu item is the **Contact** module. This is itself switched on by default.

2. The **Powered by Drupal block** is provided by the core **System** module.

By default, the Toolbar module displays links to top-level items from the core Administration menu of which, in a standard install, there is only one: **Administration** which itself comprises: **Content, Structure, Appearance, Extend, Configuration, People, Reports,** and **Help.**

Other modules have the opportunity to add extra links at any level with associated icons.

Let's experiment a little with it now, to illustrate some key navigation points. Click on the **Manage** link to show/hide the default set in the **Tray** which houses the Administration menu as follows:

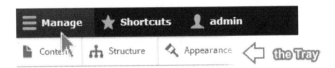

Repositioning the tray

You can easily toggle the position of the Tray between horizontal and vertical modes by clicking on the position toggle icon at the far right-hand side:

We'll now step through each item in the tray (although not in quite the order that you see them presented on the screen), and cover the basic features provided by each. Before we do that, let's first introduce three key ideas:

Responsiveness

The `Bartik` theme that we talked about in *Chapter 3, Basic Concepts*, like all modern Drupal 8 themes, is designed to be responsive and so reacts to the size of the browser viewing the page using **breakpoints**. The breakpoints are designed for the desktop (wide), tablet (standard), and mobile (narrow) browser widths.

Let's test that out now.

With the tray still visible, gradually resize your browser and you will see two things happen. At the first breakpoint, you will see the **Main menu** change shape. Try it now.

At the second breakpoint, you'll see two more significant changes.

The **Search** and **Tools** blocks both clear so that they fit nicely within a portrait smartphone screen and the items within the **Tray** itself also clear and reposition themselves on the left-hand side of the screen.

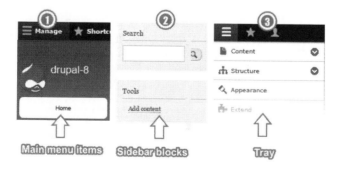

Administration theme

As we mentioned earlier in *Chapter 3, Basic Concepts* , when you visit any administration type page on your site (any path beginning with /admin/), Drupal switches to the standard profile admin theme, **Seven**.

From the home screen, click on **Manage** and then click on the **Content** link.

You will be taken to the content page, which displays in the **Seven** admin theme. To get back to the main site, click on the Back to site link in the top left-hand corner of the screen.

Now that we have those two key ideas covered, we can take a quick tour of the main administration pages of a standard Drupal 8 install.

Contextual links

Drupal's **contextual links** provide you with immediate access to edit content and configuration without having to go and visit a backend admin screen.

The **Contextual link trigger** icons appear whenever you hover your mouse pointer over an item of content to which you have the rights to perform any kind of action such as configuring a block or editing content.

Try this:

1. Hover your mouse pointer over the **Search** block, and you'll see a contextual trigger.
2. Click on the trigger (pencil) icon, and you'll see the only relevant contextual link which is shown is one to configure that block.

You can place the whole session into edit mode by clicking on the pencil (**3**) at the right-hand end of the toolbar as shown in the following screenshot.

This will reveal all the contextual link triggers (**4**) across the whole page showing exactly which parts you have in-line control over:

Quick content creation

An appreciation of this section will be much more effective if you have at least a small amount of content created so to that end let's create a couple of items of content with some *lorem ipsum* filler text and tag them with some makeshift keywords.

 There are a variety of free *Lorem Ipsum* filler text browser plugins around which can help you to speed up the process of inserting filler text. For even more fun, we recommend the *Corporate ipsum* Chrome plugin, which provides paragraphs of corporate marketing nonsense.

Don't concern yourself with the fine detail here, just follow the steps as follows:

Click on the **Shortcuts** button in the Toolbar and choose **Add content**.

Next, click on **Article** to create a new article and enter a **Title** for the article, some filler text for the **Body**, and add a couple of **tags**: 'tag1' and 'tag2'.

Finally, click on **Save and publish** at the bottom of the screen to publish the article.

You'll be taken to the default view of article with a comment form directly underneath.

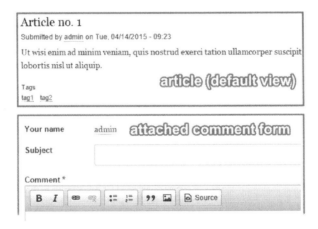

Repeat the same steps again for Article no. 2 and this time, tag the article with tag1 and tag2 as before but also add a couple of more tags such as tag3 and tag4:

You should end up with at least two Articles of content on your new site, two of which share at least two tags.

Try clicking on the tag links for Article no. 2, to see the effect of this basic tagging.

Listing content

Click on the **Content** link under **Manage** again, and you will see a list of all content that you have created so far.

You can filter content according to its **Published status** and by content **Type** and **Title**. Thus, you can easily reduce the list down to, for example, only show Articles.

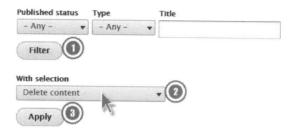

You can then select one or more items using the checkboxes and apply various actions using the **With selection** menu.

At this stage we are only aiming that you visit this page to witness the kind of bulk operations that you can do to your content nodes.

Don't actually select any of the nodes and apply any of the **With selection** options just yet and be sure to leave the articles promoted to the front page.

You may also note that you can create new content from this page too, and you'll be covering this in full detail later in *Chapter 5, Basic Content*.

Revisiting the home page

Return to your home page by clicking on the **Back to site** link followed by the Drupal logo or the **Home** menu item.

Alternatively, you can get there by typing `http://drupal-8.dd:8083` directly in the browser address bar.

Note that you can also jump straight to the home page by clicking on the site name.

You may recall from the illustration earlier, in the section entitled **Front Page**, that the **Front page Main content** region is actually a **view**. When you first visited your home page at the beginning of this chapter, you hadn't created any content, but now that you have, the dedicated Front page view lists out all the Articles that have been **Promoted to the front page** in reverse order of their creation date. By default, all the newly created Article nodes are Promoted to the front page, so you should see the following listing of teasers to your recently created articles:

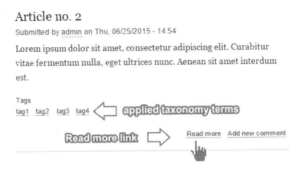

Structure

This section provides access to the all the key administrative screens for site building:

You'll be covering each section of this page more comprehensively in later chapters so we won't worry about fine detail here.

As a Drupal site builder, you'll be spending a lot of time in here and so it is well worth a quick look around the various pages to get an idea of what this section contains.

Block layout

You'll recall from *Chapter 3, Basic Concepts*, that most Drupal pages are actually made up of collections of blocks with each block being placed in a one or more theme regions.

The administration page **Manage | Structure | Block layout** provides you with a single screen to manage all the available blocks on your site. The list in the left-hand side shows you which blocks are currently active and into which regions they are placed.

You will see a list of region names and their current block content. For example, you'll see the **Site branding** block placed in the **Header** region.

You can click the **Place blocks** button to add a new block into a region and then, *when* (on which pages) they should appear according to visibility rules.

Note that the Place blocks pane is filterable and that the blocks are grouped according to whether they are: forms, lists (views), menus, system blocks, or user related:

 You can place a block as many times as you like so that you could, for example, have your search block appearing in the header and on a sidebar.

Note that the secondary tabs at the top left of the window provides access to the separate block placement pages for each of the currently enabled themes: `Bartik`, and `Seven`.

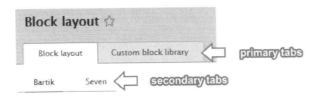

It's worth just a quick browse around the various tabs (primary and secondary) to see what is where, but as always, rest assured that guided exercises will follow later in *Chapter 6, Structure*.

Comment types

The ability for your site visitors to attach their own comments to content is a key social-publishing feature, and so in Drupal 8, you are afforded a high degree of control over when, where, and how such comments appear.

By default, in a standard installation, only the Article content type is comment enabled.

Use this structure page to dictate exactly how comment entry forms should be customized on a per-content-type basis and also how posted comments appear when browsing that content.

Comment forms can be customized in that you can add extra fields to capture different data and opt to show all or just some of these fields when the comments are later viewed attached to some actual content.

We will be covering the idea of customizing fields in detail in *Chapter 5, Basic Content*, and how to add new ones in detail in *Chapter 7, Advanced Content*, but for now, it's worth clicking on the **Manage fields** button so as to glance at the field-editing options here:

Contact forms

The Contact module provides a very useful site-wide contact form and can be configured and added to.

The **Manage** | **Structure** | **Contact Forms** link takes you to the configuration page for the Contact module.

Try editing the existing **Website feedback** category by adding in a **Recipient** address:

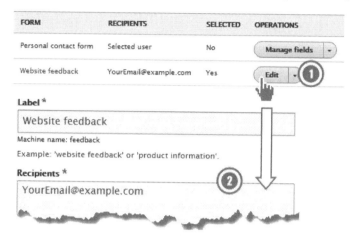

Save your changes and then visit http://drupal-8.dd:8083/contact (or click **Back to site** and then click on the existing **Contact** link in the footer menu).

Click the **Add contact form** button to add another new contact form, called **Bug report**, with its own unique URL:

Personal contact form

You can also use this contact forms configuration page to add new fields to the **Personal contact form** which, role-permitting (see later), enables site visitors to send emails directly to any other registered site users without needing to know their actual email address.

Content types

As we have seen, Drupal 8 ships with just two very basic content types: **Article** and **Basic page**. These are reasonably simple out of the box with only a few fields present but you can use the Content type administrative page at /admin/structure/types to significantly customize them by adding and configuring fields.

Customizing a content type

Visit /admin/structure/types by clicking on the **Content types** link, then use the drop-down menu to choose **Edit**.

For each content types, you can:

- Provide a human-readable name and description and also the underlying machine name.

- Provide a description of the purpose of the content type that appears on the **Manage | Structure | Content types** page.

- Set the label for Title field; the default is 'Title' but if, for example, it was a News item content type then you might want to set this to 'Headline'.

- Disable previewing of content before submission, make it mandatory to do so or make it optional.

- Specify whether content of this type, published by default, is automatically promoted to the front page and whether or not it should be marked as sticky at the top of any listings.

- Opt to display author and date information on every post of this type—ideal for news.

- Specify which, if any, Drupal menus are available for adding links to content of this type.

Customizing fields

As a Drupal site builder, you'll spend a lot of time in this administrative screen customizing your content types' fields and display settings.

We will be covering this in fine detail later in *Chapter 7, Advanced Content* but for now, it's worth a quick look at the contents of this section as a brief preview of what's to come:

1. Click on **Content types** to visit the /admin/structure/types page
2. Click on **Manage fields** button on the **Article** content type
3. Click on the **Edit** button for **Image** field in the column label **Operations**.

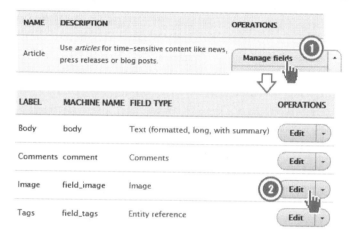

Customizing content entry screens

Access this page directly at /admin/structure/types/manage/article/form-display or via the primary tabs across the top of your screen:

You can use this admin area to edit order and behavior of the various fields when your site user is in the content-editing screen. This is referred to in Drupal as the **form display**:

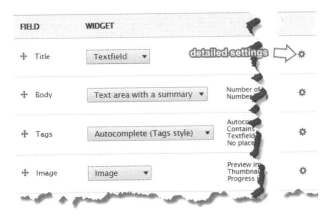

Probably, the main point of interest to you right now is the choice of widgets via which content editors can interact with the fields. As a quick exercise as to what is here, try clicking on the gear icons to the right of each field to see the configuration options that are available to you.

Full details and guided exercises are in *Chapter 7, Advanced Content*, but for now, have a quick look to see what's here.

Customizing the display

By default, the Article and Basic page content types ship with two view modes configured to control the display of those types. The **Default** is used when viewed as a whole and a shortened **Teaser** mode when the content is viewed in a listing.

In this administrative section, you are granted a lot of control over how content is displayed within these two view modes.

Click on **Manage display** and look at the **Default** view mode settings.

Note also that when you view an Article, the setting on the right-hand side controlled by the cog-wheel icon is such that any included image is automatically scaled to a predefined **Large** (480 x 480 pixel) image style:

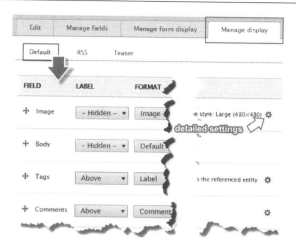

Now, click on the **Teaser** secondary tab and you should probably be able to make good sense of the settings here too.

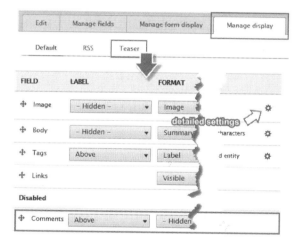

Note that when you view a **Teaser** of an Article, any included image is automatically scaled to a predefined **Medium** (220 x 220 pixels) image style and that clicking on the image is set to take you to the full piece of the content.

By default, the main **Body** copy of the article is trimmed down to 600 characters when viewed as a teaser. A default length, that in our experience, you will almost always want to reduce.

To reiterate, this section of the book only aims at giving you a basic feel for what's available here. You'll be covering the topics of customizing fields and their displays in detail in *Chapter 7, Advanced Content.*

Display modes

The term **display modes** refers to a wider grouping of how form elements are displayed in different scenarios.

There are two types of display modes: view modes (already mentioned) and form modes.

View modes

In the previous section, *Customizing the display*, you learned that we have two pre-defined view modes: Default and Teaser available for use.

We looked briefly at the differences comparing field settings and field visibility between these two, but there are actually several other inactive view modes available for content types making the full list:

- Full content
- RSS
- Search index
- Search result highlighting input
- Teaser

Likewise, there are also two view modes for users as follows:

- Compact
- User account

There are others too for different entity types such as comment, but more about these later. In *Chapter 7, Advanced C3ontent*, you'll see how you can activate/customize these and how you can set up your own custom view modes.

Form modes

Form modes are aptly named because they refer to collections of layout and configuration settings of the various relevant fields when users are filling in forms.

For example, the standard user profile edit page uses the default form display for users, but you can customize the existing **Register Form** mode so that registering a user sees a different layout when registering on the site or routinely updating their own profile.

Likewise, you can set any number of other form modes for users and employ them in different contexts throughout the site. In summary, you have a high degree of control over the default presentation of content when it is being viewed or edited. You can create any number of new **view modes** and **form modes** to suit your site's needs.

Once again, we'll cover Display modes in more detail and with practical exercises in *Chapter 7, Advanced Content*.

Menus

Drupal 8 ships with five standard menus:

- Administration
- Footer
- Main navigation
- Tools
- User account menu

Access this page directly at `admin/structure/menu` or click on the **Menus** link from the structure page:

This will take you to a page where you can edit any of the existing menus and component links, as well as create new custom menus:

TITLE	DESCRIPTION	OPERATIONS
Administration	Contains links to administrative tasks.	Edit menu ▾
Footer	Use this for linking to site information.	Edit menu ▾
Main navigation	Use this for linking to the main site sections.	Edit menu ▾
Tools	Contains links for site visitors. Some modules add their links here.	Edit menu ▾
User account menu	Links related to the user account.	Edit menu ▾

Try clicking on the **Edit menu** button next for the **Main navigation** menu and then edit the existing **Home** item.

Note that this is a special item and you can cannot actually edit it—it simply points to the default Drupal front page which, you may remember, is a list of Teasers of all items that have been Promoted to the front page.

Try the same exercise for the **Contact** entry in the **Footer** menu. Again, you will find that this item is similarly protected.

Detailed exercises with menus are in *Chapter 6, Structure*.

Taxonomy

You may recall from *Chapter 3, Basic Concepts*, that Drupal ships with a single taxonomy in place, the **Tags** vocabulary.

You'll also recall that in the earlier section, *Quick content creation*, you created two Article nodes and tagged the first with two tags: **tag1** and **tag2**, and the second with two additional ones: **tag3** and **tag4**.

These four taxonomy terms are written into the vocabulary as you entered them.

Thus, if you click on the **list terms** button, you should see those terms in place.

The administrative page at **Manage | Structure | Taxonomy** lists out all the available vocabularies and provides links for you to edit terms associated with them:

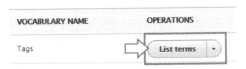

Clicking on any of the terms listed here will take you through to a page that lists out all the content that is tagged with that term:

Views

You'll recall from *Chapter 3*, *Basic Concepts*, that we pointed out that almost every Drupal site uses the **Views** module to provide filtered, grouped, and sorted lists.

The administrative page at **Manage | Structure | Views** lists out all the currently defined Views split into two distinct groups: those that are enabled and active and those are not:

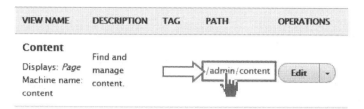

You'll be dealing with Views in detail in *Chapter 6*, *Structure*, so no need for you to dig too deep now, but what is interesting though is that one of the listed Views is entitled **Content** (see the preceding screenshot).

This View actually defines what you saw on the Content administration page back in the Listing Content section. Try clicking on the link.

Configuration

This takes you to an administrative page where you'll find configuration settings for the whole site broken down into nine categories.

We will not attempt to step though each of these here, now, but instead visit them in the context of other chapters most notably *Chapter 8*, *Configuration*

Click on the **Site information** link in the **SYSTEM** category:

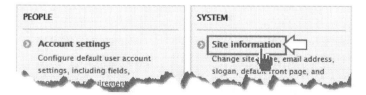

Use this link now to change the name of your site to **My Drupal Agency** or something similar. While you're there, add a slogan too. Then, save the settings and return to the site to see the effect of your configuration changes.

Appearance

Next, we'll go back into the Main Administration menu and visit the **Appearance** page:

This link takes to an administrative page where you can browse all themes and instantly switch your site into any of those available.

When you visit the page, you'll note that the currently active (default theme) is Bartik.

The other currently enabled theme is Seven and that is in use as the current administration theme and when create and editing content.

If you scroll down to the bottom of the page, you will also see an area labeled **Uninstalled themes** which currently only contains Stark.

The Stark theme is designed to show you what the raw Drupal HTML markup will look like without any kind of style applied.

Try clicking on the **Install and set as default** link to see it in action:

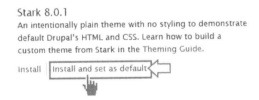

Having set Stark as the default, you'll need to click on the **Back to site** link in Toolbar to see it in action because the screen that you are currently on is an administrative page and is therefore using the Seven theme.

Having witnessed **Stark** in action, click on **Appearance** again and switch back to Bartik by clicking its **Set as default** link.

Finally, at the very bottom of the page you'll note that the Administration theme is currently set to Seven. There are no other administration themes supplied with the standard profile installation.

People

This is the default user-management page; it enables you to add new users, lists all users according to filtered criteria, and edit existing user account details:

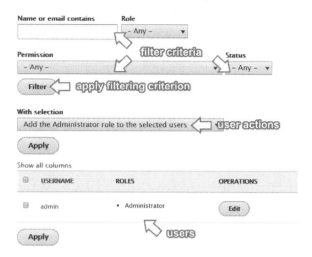

You can also apply a number of actions to the currently selected user(s).

Like any administrative screens, the **People** page is actually powered by a **View** and so, as you will see later in *Chapter 6, Structure*, you can customize the screen just as you like.

We will also be covering user management again in depth in *Chapter 9, Users and Access Control*.

Reports

The **Reports** page lists out links to a useful set of reports:

Note that when you are on any page (not just **Report** pages), you'll see a small star symbol at the end of the page's title. If you click this link, then the current page will be added to your **Shortcuts**. For example, visit the **Status report** page now and click on the star symbol sign:

From now on, access to that page will be instantly accessible from your list of shortcuts:

Extend

Last but not least in our quick tour of the Drupal 8 UI, let's visit the **Extend** page which lists out all the modules that are currently available to your site: core, contrib, and custom, their versions and whether or not they are currently active.

By default, when you first visit the page, all the module packages are expanded but if you click on any package heading, then the group will collapse.

Try this out now by collapsing all the packages:

The Drupal 8 modules page has a live, interactive search feature.

To try this out, type `Views` into the **Search** box:

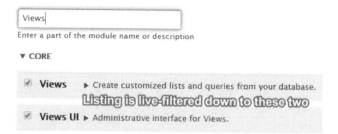

Summary

This chapter introduced some key UI terminology and introduced you to the numerous ways that you can quickly customize the UI. If you find this quite a bit to take in at once, don't worry as each of the topics is covered in greater depth in forthcoming chapters.

In the next chapter, we will introduce a site-building scenario that will help you understand the different elements of Drupal 8 using real-life examples.

5
Basic Content

In this chapter, we will introduce the site-building scenario that we will use as a vehicle for learning throughout the rest of this book. Think of this as a project brief from a new client (except without a budget).

We will be building on this scenario in each of the future chapters, improving on your Drupal 8 knowledge as we do.

Introducing your site-building scenario

Your site-building scenario is to set up a simple website for your own small business which specializes in offering a number of Drupal-specific digital services.

Types of content

The simple website will include the following types of content:

Pages

The website comprises pages which contain rich text, embedded images, and links to other areas of the site.

Pages need to be directly linked from within the Main navigation menu.

Articles

The Article content type will be used to implement the general articles, blog, and news features on the site.

Whether or not a particular article node is deemed to be a general article, blog post, or a news item will be specified by using a Category Taxonomy of either 'Articles', 'Blog posts', or 'News'.

Additionally, articles can be free tagged with one or more words or phrases from an organic collection of categorizing terms or 'Tags'.

Articles can be illustrated with images.

Articles should be comment-enabled so that users of the site can contribute to threaded conversations much as one would expect in a forum. All comments by anonymous site visitors should be directed into a moderation queue before being published.

There is no requirement for site visitors to preview comments before submitting them.

News articles should all be accessible from a news listing page.

Likewise, blogs should be listed on the blog page and general articles on an articles page.

All three lists should be sorted with the most recently created at the top of the list down to the oldest at the bottom.

Clients

Client profiles should provide a summary description of each of your clients, a logo and some client contact details in the form of an e-mail address and a telephone number.

Additionally, you should to be able to categorize each client within a work area.

The website should provide a dedicated page which lists all of your clients, grouped according to their work area classification.

Services

The site should provide a brief summary of each of the services you offer and you should be able to categorize each one in one or more work areas.

You should be able to optionally link each Service to one or more Clients.

Testimonials

The website should include a list of testimonials and each testimonial should be linked to an existing Client. There should be a dedicated page which lists testimonials grouped according to their work area classification and then sorted from newest to oldest with each group.

The testimonials should include the writer's name, job description, and company.

FAQs

The website should provide a page that lists Frequently Asked Questions (FAQs) grouped into work areas.

Contact information

The website should include a dedicated contact page where you can include details of your location as an address and a simple contact through which the public can submit enquiries.

The contact page should direct site visitors to e-mail addresses and telephone numbers for dedicated customer advisers.

We'll use the above scenario website as a vehicle for introducing new ideas and concepts from here on in this book and we'll illustrate how you might go about using Drupal 8 to achieve your ends step-by-step.

SEO considerations

The site should use Search Engine Optimized (SEO) URLs.

For example, when visiting a news item, the site should use a pattern like this:

Basic pages

In this chapter, we will focus on just the core content types: **Article** and **Basic page**.

We'll discuss step by step how to create content of these types and how to adjust their settings.

Let's imagine for argument's sake that you want create the following pages:

- Home
- Our Services
- Our Clients
- Contact us

- About us
- News
- Blog

With this in mind, let's go about creating these pages and linking them into the Main Navigation menu.

Right now, you are going to see how to create basic 'container' pages that come with nothing more than a single rich text area in which you can add your content. Later, in *Chapter 6, Structure*, you will see how you can include blocks within these pages too. For example, the news page should list out all of the news items.

We already have a home page link so let's start with the **Our services** page.

Creating a new page

To create a new Basic page, navigate to **Shortcuts | Add content | Basic page**.

On the left-hand side, we have the main area, which is where you get to populate the various fields of the basic page content type:

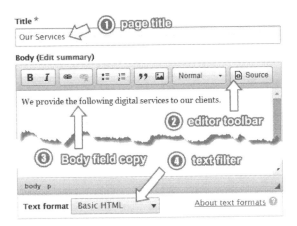

Title

Enter `Our Services` in the **Title** field.

Body

Enter some introductory text as shown earlier, but don't actually save the content yet.

Body field summary

You may have noticed the **Edit summary** link just to the right of the **Body** field's label.

Understanding the significance of this with respect to good **Search Engine Optimization (SEO)** is quite important, so let's look for a moment at how the summary gets used when the content is presented in a summarized (teaser) form.

When Drupal provides information in a summarized format, it applies the rules:

- If the Summary of the Body field is populated, then Drupal will use the content intelligently, truncating it at a predetermined length if it is too long

- In the absence of a populated Summary, Drupal will fall back to intelligently truncating the Body content itself.

To illustrate this in action, edit the **Our Services** page and add some summary text:

Then, even though the Body text is populated, the teaser would appear:

You won't be able to see this action for yourself unless you have covered either manually promoting content to the front page in *Chapter 4, Getting Started with the UI* or done the Views work in *Chapter 6, Structure*, but for now, take my word for it that it's always worth taking time out to populate these Summary elements with concise descriptions.

Rich text toolbar

Drupal 8 employs a WYSIWYG (What You See Is What You Get) JavaScript editor to provide for a rich text editing toolbar.

Default HTML restrictions

Note that by default, Drupal 8 ships with the Basic **Body** field configured to filter the rich text according to a set of rules limiting the HTML tags. The allowed tags are those defined in the **Basic HTML** Text format.

Note how the WYSIWYG editor toolbar for this particular text format is also equipped with only the right set of icons to match the restricted set of HTML tags.

The **Basic HTML** text format provides a basic toolbar:

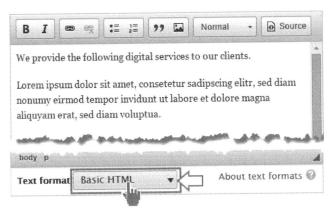

One of the default rules restricts the possible tags to those in the following list:

```
<a> <em> <strong> <cite> <blockquote> <code> <ul> <ol> <li> <dl> <dt>
<dd> <h4> <h5> <h6> <p> <span> <img>
```

Full HTML

By contrast, this text format provides the full set of HTML tags to be used and therefore comes with a much busier toolbar.

Restricted HTML

This restricts the user to the same list as for Basic HTML, but excludes the `<span>` and `<img>` tags. It also removes the rich toolbar.

 Try changing the Text format between the available options, both with and without text in place to see various messages and their effects on the **Body** field.

In either Basic HTML or Full HTML, you'll also note that one of these toolbar icons is the **Source** switcher, which allows you to switch out of the rich editing mode and instead manipulate the HTML directly:

One should not be misled here into thinking that if you switch to the **Source** editing mode, you are no longer restricted in terms of the HTML tags that you can use. This is not so; Drupal actually performs the filtering on output not the input so that you can actually enter any old HTML into the **Body** field while in Source mode, but only the allowed tags list (above) will actually be output.

 Configuring the application of different text formats to different content types is a key feature for avoiding the situation where clients may have too much freedom to enter custom HTML, which may well break the website's layout.

Adding a page to the main navigation menu

Next, cast your eye over to the advanced editing area on the right-hand side where you will find an expandable field set entitled **MENU SETTINGS**.

Expanding this area will enable you to enter a title for the menu entry:

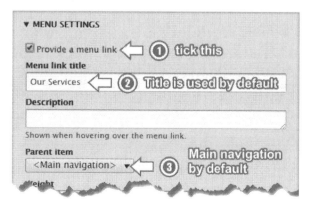

Ensure the **Provide a menu link** checkbox is selected, and then enter a title — Our Services. Make a mental note that the default **Parent item** is automatically set to <Main navigation> and then **Save and publish** the page:

You should now be viewing your finished page and see that it is conveniently displayed in the Main navigation menu.

Nodes and unique IDs

All content on a Drupal website is stored and treated as "nodes". The node is a terminology that has persisted throughout Drupal's long history. It is less important in Drupal 8 where you will hear discussion of "entities" more often than nodes. Suffice to say that a node is any posting of content such as a Basic page or Article.

By saving the new Basic page, you have just created your first node. In fact, assuming that you are following this tutorial guide to the letter, you have just created a node with a unique ID of 3 because you created nodes 1 and 2 back in *Chapter 4, Getting Started with the UI.*

Hover over the **Edit** tab (**2**) and glance at your browser's status line where you should be able to see the **Edit** link drupal-8.dd:8083/node/3/edit.

Note that the pattern of this URL ends with /node/[nid]/edit where [nid] is the unique **node ID** of the node you have just created.

 The node ID is often shortened to nid in Drupal parlance. You will see references to nid repeatedly during your Drupal journey.

Adding more pages

Next, using the same techniques, add the following further Basic pages to your site, each with a small amount of filler text and a Main navigation menu item:

- **Our Clients**
- **Contact us**
- **About us**
- **News**

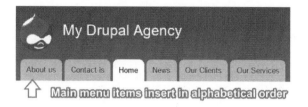

 Note that Drupal 8 automatically orders the menu items in alphabetical order, but also note that you can easily rearrange these as you will see in *Chapter 6, Structure*.

So, you now have a working website with five pages; not overly impressive, but a good start.

Let's look at Articles again to see how they differ from Basic pages.

Articles

The only other Content type that is available out of the box with Drupal 8 is the Article.

We touched on this content type earlier in *Chapter 4, Getting Started with the UI*, but that was only in a simple example. This time you'll look at them in more detail.

Creating a new article

To create a new Article, navigate to **Shortcuts | Add content | Article**.

Let's look at the extra fields you get with an Article that didn't appear when we created Basic pages earlier. You'll create an article about the company pet as a vehicle for investigating what's different about Articles nodes.

In addition to the **Title** and **Body** fields, the Article caters for categorizing the article content using one or more "tags", and it also provides an image field so that you can attach an image to the article.

Add a **Title** and some **Body** text:

Tag the article with a couple of keywords:

Finally, upload a suitable picture (the exact one here is available in the book resource ZIP file), and add an image with accompanying Alt-text for accessibility.

Note the alt text is compulsory forcing you to follow accessibility best-practices.

Click on the **Save and publish** button to publish the article, and it should appear:

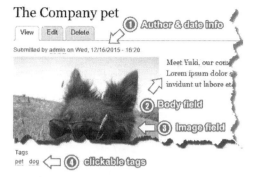

Note some key points about Articles compared with Basic pages:

- The author and date information is displayed at the top of the page
- The image is automatically resized from the original—more about how in *Chapter 8, Configuration*
- Tags are clickable, and will take you to a page of similarly tagged content

Now create a second article with some similar content, and tag that with the word dog.

Having saved the second article, try clicking on the **dog** tag at the bottom of the page:

You should see that Drupal takes you to a listing of **teaser** (shortened) versions of all content that is tagged with the same tag, with the most recently created at the top:

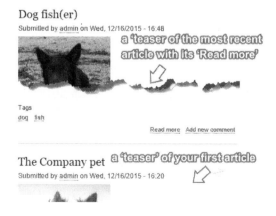

Note that the **Edit** tab located at the top of the page is an edit shortcut to the dog tag itself and not one for the first article in this. You might like to click on the **Edit** link just to see this for yourself:

In this simple example, you can already see the enormous power inherent in being able to display categorized content in this way.

Thus, you can see that Drupal is already proving its worth by providing a useful summary of all content throughout the site, which is similarly tagged. Imagine if, instead of just these two articles about pets, you had a large range of clothing products tagged with "shoes".

Front page promotion

Visit your site home page now by clicking on either the **Home** link in the Main navigation menu or the site logo:

You may be forgiven for thinking that you are looking at the same view as before, that is, a teaser listing of everything tagged with dog. However, what you are actually looking at is a teaser listing of all articles, at least all articles that have been **Promoted to front page**.

So why are we seeing all these articles? The answer is that, by default, the Article content type is **Promoted to front page** and the default Drupal front page displays up to ten of them in reverse order of creation date and time.

Demote your **Dog fish(er)** article. Remember that in addition to the **Edit** tab, you can use the contextual links for quick editing:

Dog fish(er)

Submitted by admin on Wed, 12/16/2015 - 16:48

Locate the **Promotional options** in the advanced editing area and un-tick **Promote to front page** (2) before resaving the Article node (3).

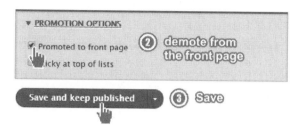

Your **Dog fish(er)** article will no longer appear as a teaser on the front page.

 I'll remind you that you can also demote multiple items of content from the front page at `admin/content` using bulk actions as you saw back in *Chapter 4, Getting Started with the UI*.

Adjusting the settings for a content type

Drupal gives you complete control over the default settings for each content type, and we'll now illustrate how to make site-wide adjustments to the behavior of any of them quickly and easily through the administrative interface.

Disabling front page promotion

While it is a useful default feature that Drupal automatically promotes Article nodes to the front page, let's imagine that we have a plan to provide a list of article teasers another way (almost certainly using Views) and so wish to turn off the automatic facility.

 Note that once we have this setting adjustment in place, it will only affect the behavior of all new articles.

To adjust the settings for the content type as a whole, locate the **Content types** link from the **Structure** page.

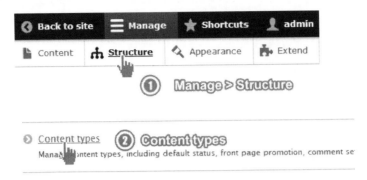

Next, choose **Edit** to edit the **Article** content type as a whole by dropping down the **Operations** menu:

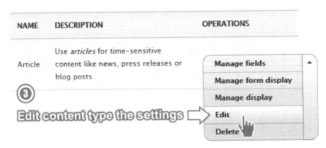

In the following dialog, locate the **Publishing options** section and uncheck the **Promote to front page** option and save the settings:

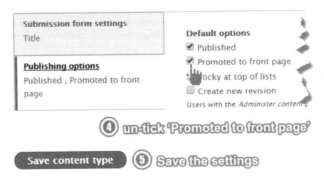

You have now configured your site such that all the newly created articles are no longer automatically promoted to the front page.

Note that the same set of default content type settings are available for adjustment for all content types such as core, contributed, and your own custom types, as you will see later in *Chapter 7, Advanced Content*.

Adjusting comment settings

Let's now adjust the settings for the Article content type so that articles do not, by default, have comment forms attached to them. This will involve your first visit to the field management page for the article content type—a key area to get to grips with when configuring the various types of content on your Drupal site.

We have two distinct possibilities:

- Keep any existing comments, but disable all comments on the newly created content

- Remove the ability to leave comments for all Articles and remove all comment data

The first involves adjusting the settings for the **Comment** field, and the second involves the complete removal of the **Comment** field from the Article content type.

Either way, to adjust the settings for the content type, again locate the **Content types** link from the **Structure** page by navigating to **Manage | Structure | Content types**.

Next, choose **Manage** fields for the Article type:

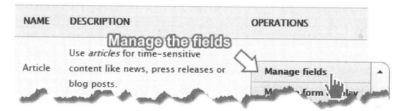

You will be taken to a page that shows the different fields that make up the Article content type.

Disabling future comments

In the first example, you'll adjust the settings of the **Comment** field so that no further comments can be added to the article nodes; this will have the effect of removing the comment form from all newly created articles, but will leave it on any pre-existing nodes. Comments that already exist will be retained.

Locate the menu on the right-hand side of **Comments** and click on the **Edit** option:

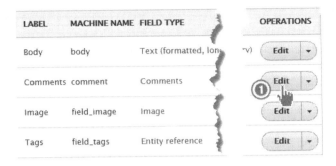

You will be taken to the **Comment** field settings page.

Locate the **Default Value** field settings about half way down the page and click on the radio button labeled **Hidden**.

Save the settings.

No retrospective action

It's important to be clear that having hidden comments in the default field settings for the article content type, you will no longer see the comment form on *new* articles.

Existing articles, comment settings are unaffected by changes to the default field settings. So, the existing comments and more importantly, the comment entry form will still show any existing articles enabling user to continue adding comments and replying to existing ones.

Retrospective action

By contrast, the other settings found in the **COMMENT FORM SETTINGS** area do apply retrospectively; these are:

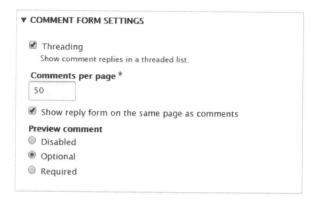

Threading

Comment **threading** means that replies to comments and indeed replies to replies will all be indented so as to show visually how the individual threads of conversation have progressed:

Thus, if you uncheck the **Threading** option, then replies to comments will no longer be indented so as to show the various conversation threads.

Show reply form on the same page as comments

This option controls whether the comment entry form is automatically attached to the bottom of every comment-equipped article or whether it instead presents a simple text link:

Once un-ticked and the settings saved, the full comment form will no longer show and will be replaced by a much neater **Add new comment** link:

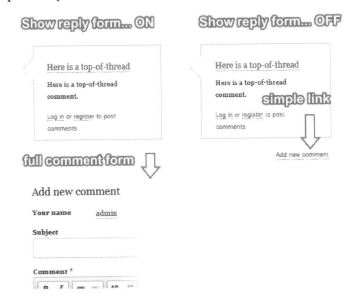

Use the preceding idea now to configure Articles to display the simple link as shown in the preceding screenshot.

Preview comments before posting

Similarly, you can opt to allow your site users to preview their comment(s) before posting them, and you can even force them to preview before they can post:

Removing all comments and the ability to comment

We are not actually going to do this now, but if we have no intention of using comments on articles on the site and we don't mind removing any exiting comment data, then another approach is to remove the **Comments** field altogether.

You can remove the field from the field management page by clicking on the down arrow next to the **Edit** operation and selecting **Delete**.

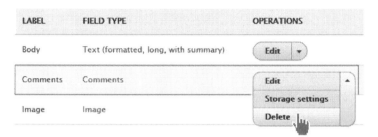

Note that the action of removing the field is permanent and cannot be undone; you will lose all the comment data associated with articles, so use with care in real projects.

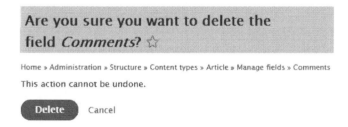

It's fine to do so; you can always add the field back in later if you change your mind about allowing comments on the Article content type.

Summary

In this chapter, we introduced the basic plan for your new site and we started creating real pages and articles. We looked in some detail at the key features of the fields available within the Basic page and Article content types, and in particular, how to adjust the settings on the comment field.

Equipped with these new skills, you should be ready to start creating new content types and customizing them exactly as you need to implement Clients, Services, Testimonials, and FAQs on your new site in *Chapter 7, Advanced Content*. First, let's look into some more of the key structural elements of Drupal: Menus, Taxonomy, Views, and Blocks in the next chapter.

6

Structure

In this chapter, we will be looking at organizing the structure of content on your Drupal website. To start with, we'll look at menus before investigating taxonomy in more depth than in our earlier introduction. Finally, we will take a look at creating lists of data as pages and blocks using the Views module.

Managing menus

The representation of the structure of your site to a user will often be via menus. Here we will show you how to manipulate these menus so that you can help a user navigate your site.

Reorganizing menu items

As it stands, our **Main navigation menu** items are listed in alphabetical order:

However, we would like the items in the following order:

Home | Our Services | Our Clients | About us | News | Contact us

To edit the menu, visit the Menu management at **Manage | Structure | Menus**:

You will see a list of all the currently defined menus; try editing the Main navigation menu:

Use the 'drag handles' to reorder the menu items:

Rearrange the order and save so that your **Main navigation** menu appears like this:

Editing menu items

Earlier, we made a dedicated **Contact us** Basic page and we linked it into the **Main navigation** menu at the same time. To illustrate the idea of editing menu items manually, let's point this menu item to the existing Contact form that was automatically provided to us by the `Contact` module instead of the Basic page.

Even though the menu item was created at the time of creating the page, we can easily overwrite the location that it points to. You may remember from *Chapter 4, Getting Started with the UI*, that the Contact module provides a contact form at `http://drupal-8.dd:8083/contact`.

Visit the Menu management page again by navigating to **Manage | Structure | Menus | Main navigation**.

In order to have the Contact us menu item point to the form instead of the Basic page, all you need to do is manually edit the menu item by clicking on the **Edit** button in the **OPERATIONS** column.

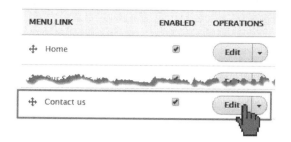

The **Menu link title** is simply the text attached to the menu item (**1**) but the **Link**, in our case the **Contact us** Basic page, is neatly disguised as the title of that targeted page with the nid in brackets afterward:

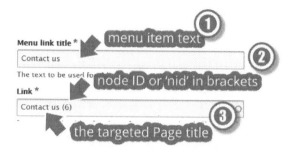

Edit the item's **Link** replacing the existing reference to your Contact page (the Basic page with a node ID of 6) with the replacement path of /contact, which is provided by the Contact module.

To manually enter a relative path such as this, precede the path with a forward slash (/).

Save your changes.

Since you are no longer linking the Main navigation menu to the Basic page you created in *Chapter 4, Getting Started with the UI*, we could remove that page but in fact, we'll keep it and use it later to demonstrate some other features.

Managing taxonomy

In *Chapter 3, Basic Concepts*, we briefly discussed Drupal's Taxonomy feature.

In *Chapter 4, Getting Started with the UI*, you created Article nodes tagged with the terms: tag1, tag2, tag3, and tag4, and in *Chapter 5, Basic Content*, you created more Article nodes tagged with the terms pet and dog.

The **Tags** vocabulary is a **tag-based vocabulary**, which means that content editors can make up as many terms (words or phrases) as they like and will be prompted to re-use any existing terms as they type. Tag-based vocabularies are great when you need your content-editing team to use their expert subject knowledge to build up a collection of terms, but the downside of them is that the collections can fill up with duplication owing to misspellings.

> Taxonomy vocabularies based on a fixed set of terms are often more useful. What we will do next is set up a fixed vocabulary to help us to categorize all the content (pages, services, clients, and news) across the site.

Creating a new Taxonomy vocabulary

We'll create the following collection of seven terms that we can use to categorize all content:

- Charities
- Consultancy
- Documentation
- E-Commerce
- Government
- Fun
- Training

We'll refer to this as the *Category* vocabulary.

To create a brand new taxonomy vocabulary for our new list of terms, visit **Structure | Taxonomy | Add vocabulary**.

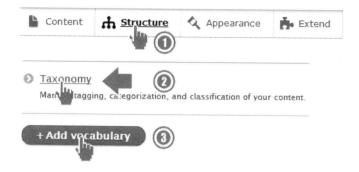

Enter a name and description for the new vocabulary and save it.

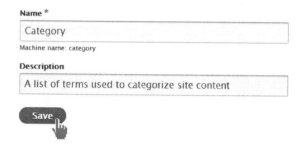

Click on the **Add term** link and start entering all the terms in the list.

Note that whilst we have done so in the screenshot below to illustrate the feature, you do not need to enter an administrative **Description** for each and every term.

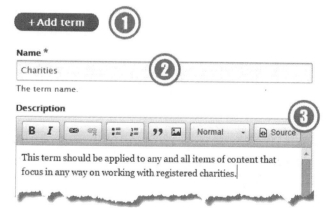

Enter the full list of terms as follows:

- Charities
- Consultancy
- Documentation
- E-Commerce
- Fun
- Government
- Training

Re-ordering Taxonomy terms

Since you have only just populated the vocabulary from scratch, you will find that the terms in it are already arranged in alphabetical order.

It is a common requirement to list out taxonomy terms in a precise curated order, and so you can simply drag and drop the various terms until you have what you want.

Visit the **Manage | Structure | Taxonomy** page and click on the **List** tab.

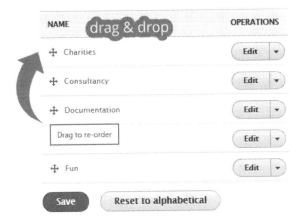

Apply a taxonomy vocabulary to content types

Now that you have defined the new list of terms with which to classify the website content, the next step is to associate the vocabulary to your existing content types: Basic page and Article. To do this, we need to add a field to each of those content types. Let's first attach the vocabulary to the Article content type.

Go to **Manage | Structure | Content types** then click on the **Manage Fields** button in the operations dropdown for the Article content type:

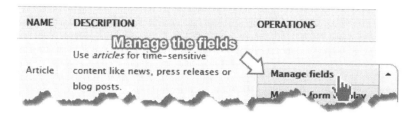

Add a new **Reference | Taxonomy term** field called `Category` and **Save and continue**:

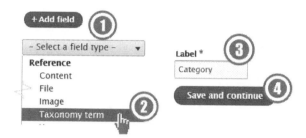

You will then be taken to the first of two field configuration pages.

Let's say that we want to allow the content editors to have the option to apply multiple terms, so select **Unlimited** as the first option, and then make sure that the field is linked up to the correct (Category) taxonomy vocabulary:

Finally, you'll be taken to the second field configuration screen where you can optionally make the field mandatory, set any default value(s), and finalize the settings such as whether to limit the vocabularies you wish to use or to set any default terms.

At the bottom of the configuration screen, use the **Default** reference method and make sure that only the **Category** vocabulary is selected:

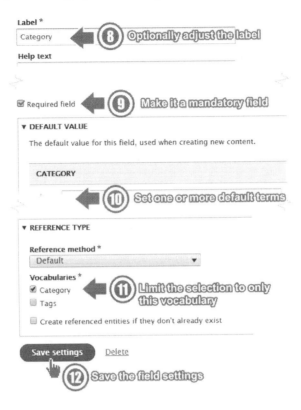

Leave **Create references entities if they don't already exist** unticked, otherwise new terms will be created in this vocabulary and it will essentially become a tag type vocabulary when this is selected.

When creating and editing articles, your content-editing team will now be able to categorize their content.

Before we test this out, let's first use the opportunity to visit another field configuration page again—that of **Manage form display**.

Adjusting the order of fields when editing

We touched on this in *Chapter 4, Getting Started with the UI*; now let's look at it in a bit more detail. As a reminder, when we use the word **Form** in Drupal in relation to editing content, we are referring to the **Edit form,** that is, the actual screen which the content editors use to edit content.

Visit the **Manage form display** screen for the Article content type. Click on **Manage form display** from the operations dropdown:

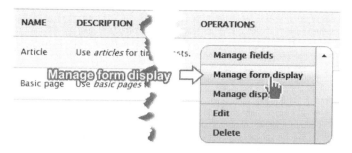

The most intuitive widget that we can use would be a **Select list,** so let's configure the field to use that when in the edit form.

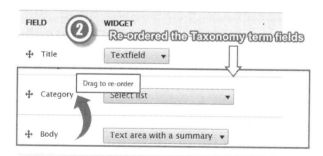

You should leave the **Tags** field widget set to the default **Autocomplete** since that is the only really sensible open for a tags vocabulary.

It is often a good idea to bring Taxonomy term fields to the top of the list just underneath the Title to encourage content editors to think about classification early on when they are creating new content.

Thus, re-order the fields, as shown in the following, so that the two Taxonomy fields are positioned just below the **Title**.

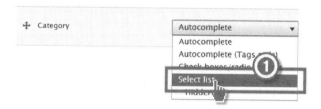

Categorizing content

Now that we have set up a link between the Article content type and the Category taxonomy, we can set about categorizing Articles.

To categorize your four existing articles, simply edit them and choose one or more terms using *Ctrl* within Windows or *Command* on OS X, and then save.

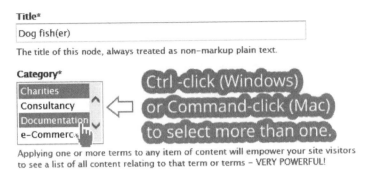

Categorize all four existing articles now for example, The company pet and Dog fish(er) articles might reasonably be categorized as Fun and so on.

Create five new articles now in a variety of categories.

You may find it useful to copy the list of titles that we have used in this tutorial guide:

- An article classified with Charities
- An article classified with Consultancy
- An article classified with Charities and Documentation
- An article classified with Consultancy and E-Commerce
- An article classified with Consultancy, Government, and Training

Note that we have not added any images to the example articles created in this guide, but you, of course, can.

Viewing categorized content

Visit one of your articles now in full and you will see that any **Category** terms that you have applied appear as links at the bottom of the page:

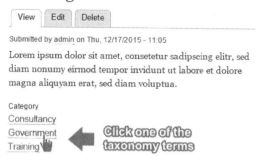

Clicking on one of these links will again take you to a listing of all content with that term applied. Not bad at all, but now let's see how we can use taxonomy to provide further improved listing.

Segregating article types using taxonomy

So far we have used taxonomy to group together articles whose actual content is concerned with key terms such as Charities, government, and Training. Now let's investigate how we can use exactly the same methods to distinguish between three different *types* of Article: Articles, News, and Blog posts.

Creating another taxonomy vocabulary

We are now going to subdivide Article nodes into three distinct types: Articles, Blog posts, and News. To do this, we first need to create a new Taxonomy vocabulary.

Visit **Manage | Structure | Taxonomy**.

Create a new vocabulary called `Article type` containing the following terms: Articles, Blog posts, and News:

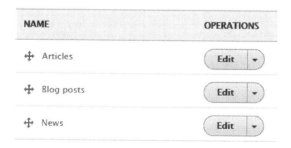

Next, in order to enable you to classify Article nodes with these terms, add another **Taxonomy term** field entitled `Article type` to your Article content type so as to attach this new vocabulary. As you do, set the **DEFAULT VALUE** of the field to **Articles** so as to classify all newly created articles as Articles by default:

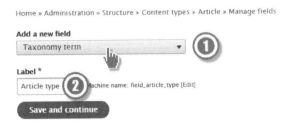

Leave the Limit set to 1 since an Article should only be of a single type:

Adjust the default value to be Articles:

Lastly, limit the choice of terms to the **Article type** vocabulary and save the settings a final time:

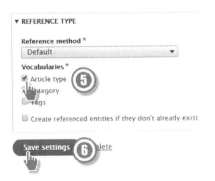

Set the widget to **Select list** and adjust the order of the fields in the **Manage form display** page to bring the new Taxonomy field close to the top of the page.

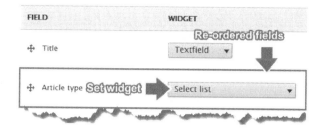

Now go through each of your existing articles further classifying with an Article type.

You may find it useful to copy the classification that we have used in this tutorial guide:

- An article classified with Charities [News]
- An article classified with Consultancy [News]
- An article classified with Charities and Documentation [News]
- An article classified with Consultancy and E-Commerce [Articles]
- An article classified with Consultancy, Government, and Training [Articles]
- The company pet, Dog fish(er), Article no. 1, and Article no. 2 [Blog posts]

Test your new classification by clicking on one of the three terms to see a nicely segregated listing showing only Articles, News, or Blog posts.

In the next section, you will see how you can improve significantly on this listing by controlling the order, grouping, and presentation of the articles using the **Views** module.

Working with the Views module

You are now in a good position to start investigating how to the use the Views module to create carefully filtered and organized listings of content that are organized just as you want.

Creating a Views-powered News page

To create a new View, visit the **Manage** | **Structure** | **Views** page:

You will see a list of all the existing views, some of which are active and some disabled:

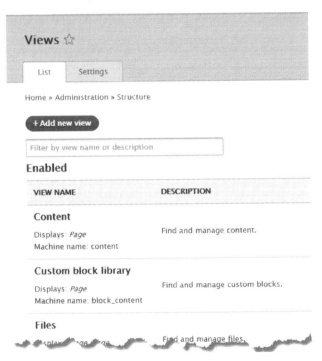

View wizard

The view wizard will help you create new views more quickly by guiding you through the common setup steps.

Creating a new view

Next, click on the **+Add new view** button and you will be taken into the Views wizard. We'll keep this explanation simple to start with by concentrating only on the elements of this screen that are essential to build the News page view.

Later in this chapter, we will go into more detail about the finer points of the Views wizard. Name the new View News and filter the content to the **Article** type.

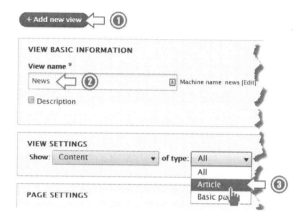

 At this point, you may be forgiven for thinking that you can also set the Tagged with field to narrow down the News page to only those Articles that are really News items because they are marked with the News term from the Article type taxonomy list and you'd be quite right. However, while the wizard is a simple starting point within this wizard, the only taxonomy vocabulary that Views is aware of at this stage is the core Tags vocabulary, and that won't do in our case.

We want to create a full page that is accessible via a unique URL path, so check the **Create a page** checkbox and check and adjust the **Page title** and a **Path** if you need to:

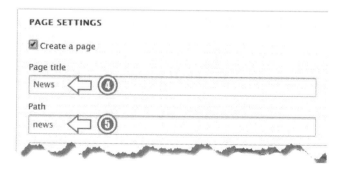

We want the News page to be accessible from the **Main navigation** menu, so also check the **Create a menu link** item and direct the link to the **Main navigation** menu:

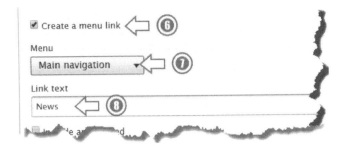

Click on the **Save and edit** button:

You will be taken into the Views editing page showing the view with one display entitled **Page**.

Renaming a display

It's worth noting at this point that Views can actually contain any number of different types of **Displays**, but more about that later in this chapter when we add a block display.

For now, though let's specifically rename the display that we have just created so that it is more descriptive. Click on the current **Display name** and rename it to News list as a Page so that it's very clear what it does.

The newly revised display name will replace the original one in the list:

Live preview

Scroll down the editing page and you'll find a live preview currently listing out all the published Article nodes. We have not yet filtered the list down to only those marked as News items, so this is correct.

Content settings

Before adding the finishing touches, let's take a look at some key **Format, Filtering,** and **Sort** settings that have been set up by the View wizard.

1. Firstly, scroll back up and look at the Format settings and note that we are displaying items in their currently defined Teaser view mode.

2. There are two Filter criteria currently applied limiting the listed items to only **Articles** that are **published**.

3. The listed items are sorted in reverse order of **Authored on** (creation) date.

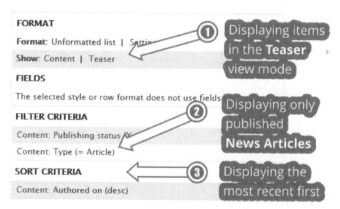

Page settings

It's worth noting at this point that if you made an error or an omission when in the wizard, you can re-adjust the path settings and, therefore, change the actual URL through which your site visitors will view the News page.

You can also adjust the **PAGE SETTINGS** for the menu item used to provide access to page and to change the actual Drupal menu in which that item is contained.

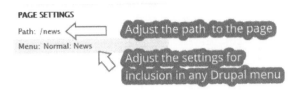

There are other useful and interesting settings here too such as the ability to control precisely who can see the results of the View based on permission(s) or role(s), and we'll cover those later.

Filtering to News only

The only thing we need to add now is to further filter down the list of Articles to only those that have their **Article type** field (a Taxonomy reference) to **News**. The following are the steps to achieve this.

1. Add a new **Filter criterion** to the view:

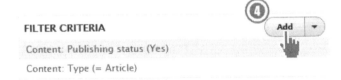

2. Enter tax in the **Search** input in order to filter down the list of possible criteria to only those relating to taxonomy.

3. Select **Has taxonomy term**.

4. Click on **Apply (all displays)**.

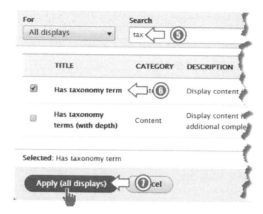

5. Next, in order to target the specific vocabulary that contains the News term, choose the **Article type** vocabulary, opting for a Dropdown widget for convenience. Click on **Apply and continue.**

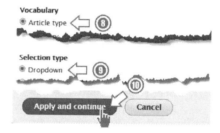

6. From the list of terms within the Article type vocabulary, choose **News** in order to filter out only those Article nodes that are marked as news items. Click on **Apply to all displays** once more and then click on **Save** (between the main editing area and the preview) to finalize the whole view.

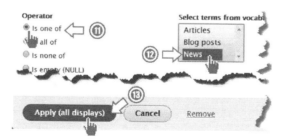

7. Finally, after you have been returned back to the underlying Views edit page, hit the Save button at the bottom left.

8. Return to the Home page and you should see two **News** pages accessible from the **Main navigation** menu: the first being the original **Basic page** that you added back in *Chapter 5, Basic Content,* and the new Views-powered **News** page that you have just created.

9. Click on the second News tab to see the Views-powered page in action. You should see a list of all Article nodes that have been categorized as "News".

Don't be tempted to remove the original Basic page from the menu right now because you are going to use it later to help illustrate the usefulness of creating Blocks using the `Views` module.

Creating a blog page

In this exercise you will create a page that lists blog posts out as teasers.

The steps to achieve this are straightforward and exactly as per the *Creating a Views-powered News page* section, but let's just recap on them as revision.

We already have some posts categorized as Blog posts.

Create a new page view entitled `Blog` that lists only Articles with the list filtered down those which are marked as **Blog post**.

If you are unsure at this point, then please look back at the **Creating a Views-powered News page** section for a step-by-step recap on building the News page.

Working with Views blocks

In the previous section, we created two entirely separate Views-powered pages to list all the **News** items and Blog posts, that is, those Article nodes that had been marked as News or Blog posts. As an illustration of the ease with which you can create separate blocks for content lists using the Views module, let's now create a block version of the news listing and place that block on the Basic page entitled News that you created in *Chapter 5*, *Basic Content*.

Creating blocks using Views

Locate the newly created Views-powered News page and hover your mouse pointer near the top of the view's output. This should reveal the contextual link for the view as a whole, allowing you to edit the view quickly and easily without even knowing its name.

Create a block version of the existing display by clicking on the **+Add** button and choosing to add a new **Block** Display.

Click on the new **Display name:** label entitled 'Block'

Rename the **Block** to **News list as a Block** as you did earlier:

Since this is a Block display and not a page that can be visited via a URL path, it does not have any Path settings but instead has some block-specific settings in the central region of the dialog. In order for the block to be visible to the block placement system, you must name the block specifically, so click on the word **None** (next to block name) now.

Set the name of the block to `News listing block` and click on **Apply**:

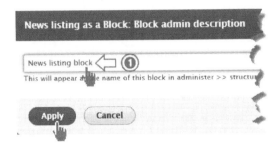

Save the view before continuing.

You have now created a new block and it will be available for placement on the Block layout page that you first saw back in *Chapter 4, Getting Started with the UI*.

Let's look again at how to do just that.

Placing the News blocks

The overall goal here is to place the new News block onto the existing News page immediately underneath the Body field.

Go to **Manage** | **Structure** | **Block layout**.

Locate the **Content** region and click the **Place block** button.

Scroll down the page to locate the newly-created block entitled **News listing block**.

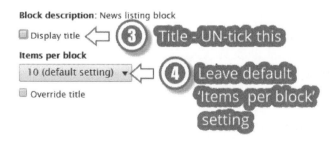

Block position

Let's place the block on the News page.

You'll concentrate only on the key points for now, which are essentially where, how, and when we want the News listing block to appear in simple steps.

We don't want the Title showing because we already have a title on the news page, so unclick **Display title.**

The default option to view 10 news items at a time seems sensible so leave that alone.

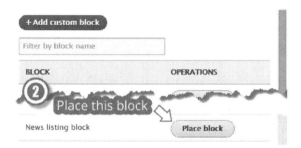

Block visibility

So that's the how and the where dealt with, we now need only to tell Drupal when we want that block to be displayed, and the criterion for that is that we are viewing the News page which, if you've been following along, will be node/7.

So, the two visibility settings that need adjusting within the collapsed **Pages** field group so as to make the block is only visible on the News page are:

Click on the left-hand side **Pages** section.

Enter /node/7.

Select the **Show for the listed pages** option:

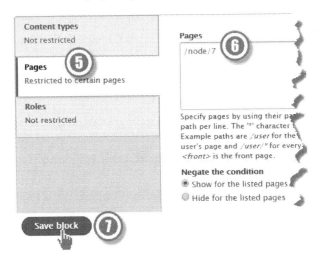

You can now re-position the **News** block directly underneath the existing Main content block and then click on **Save blocks**:

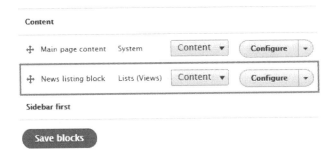

You should only see the **News** listing block when you are actually viewing the original News page (node/7) that you created back in *Chapter 5, Basic Content*.

The visible "page" now comprises the original **Basic page** and the **View** block.

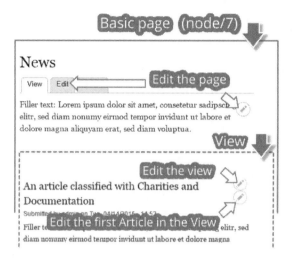

 Note that you can see multiple contextual links on the overall visible page: one for the Basic page, one for the View, and one for each News article.

Now that you have placed the **News** listing block on the **News** page, we no longer need the second menu item that was provided by the **News** Page display within the **News** View.

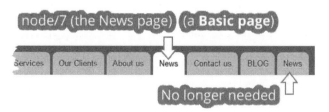

This is a good opportunity to re-visit the menu management screen and to see how, rather than deleting the item, you can just temporarily disable it instead. Likewise, we could actually remove the Page display from the News View but, again, leaving it in place will prove very useful later in *Chapter 7, Advanced Content*, when we touch on some of the more advanced features of the `Views` module.

For now, just disable the second **News** menu item – the one provided by your News view - in the Main navigation menu.

Go to **Manage | Structure | Menus**.

Edit the **Main navigation** menu, then disable the item, and save the settings.

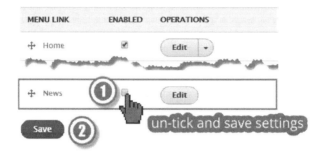

Let's finish by taking a look at what `Views` offers in terms of options for the HTML markup of its output.

Out of the box, the `Views` module offers four formats of output:

- Grid
- HTML List
- Table
- Unformatted list

Visit the **News** page (`node/7`) again and edit the news view directly using the contextual link, as shown in the following screenshot:

This should take you to the View edit screen centered on the News list as a Block display. Locate the **FORMAT** section on the left-hand side and click on the **Unformatted list** default.

As an exercise, we are going to change the output markup to be in a grid style, but we are only going to do this for the News **block** and not the News **page**.

So, in the next screen, dropdown the **For:** menu and choose **This block (override)**, which means that any changes we are about to make will only apply to the block display and not to the original Page display.

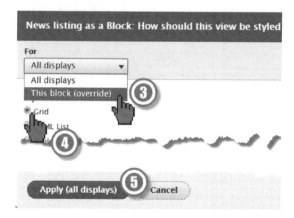

Change the style setting from **Unformatted list** to **Grid** and below and set the **Number of columns** to **2**. Apply the new settings:

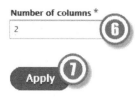

Finally, save the View:

Save the view and go and revisit the **News** page.

The news article listing should now be output as a grid of two column widths like the following:

An article classified with Documentation

Submitted by admin on Wed, 12/31/2014 - 14:43

Lorem ipsum dolor sit amet, consetetur sadipscing elitr, sed diam nonumy eirmod tempor invidunt ut labore et dolore magna aliquyam erat, sed diam voluptua.

Read more   Add new comment

An article classified with Consultancy and Government

Submitted by admin on Wed, 12/31/2014 - 14:42

Lorem ipsum dolor sit amet, consetetur sadipscing elitr, sed diam nonumy eirmod tempor invidunt ut labore et dolore magna aliquyam erat, sed diam voluptua.

Read more   Add new comment

Summary

In this chapter, we introduced some of the key ideas for managing the structure of a Drupal site. We briefly covered menu management to help provide a basic top level site navigation. Then we concentrated on employing Drupal's powerful Taxonomy system to help provide grouped lists of all of the site content according to how the content might be tagged with keywords or more specifically categorized with one or more words or phrases from fixed lists of categorizing terms. Then we looked at how you can employ taxonomy again to provide three forms of article — Article, Blog, and News — based around the basic Drupal Article content type.

We spent some time employing the powerful Views module to query the site database and building content lists based on filtering criteria and we saw how the module could be used to create both pages and blocks output. Finally, we saw some examples of the built-in formats that the Views module provides to control the markup style of its output.

In the next chapter, we will be returning to content editing and exploring some of the more advanced editing and configuration Drupal 8 has to offer.

7
Advanced Content

In this chapter, we will look more at the various field types that are available and we will present some practical exercises creating new content types that you will need to help realize the remaining functionality laid out in the site-building scenario introduced in *Chapter 5, Basic Content*.

You will experience scenarios where you might use the different field types in real site builds and cover some more tips and tricks with the Views module along the way.

Field types

Before we describe each of the core field types, let's first make sure that they are all available because by default, not all the available field type modules are active.

We'll need the **Link** and **Telephone** type fields to be active. The Link module should be enabled already, but we'll need to activate the Telephone field module.

Visit the modules listing page at **Admin | Manage | Extend**.

Scroll down to **FIELD TYPES** and enable the **Telephone** field, as shown in the following screenshot:

Extending content types

In the next section, we'll look at some common adjustments made to fields—their content-editing interfaces, prompt text, default values, and their display settings—so as to get used to the options available to you.

Adjusting field settings

We'll start by making some adjustments to the core **Article** and **Basic page** content types and then move on to creating some new content types and employing some new field types to meet the requirements as laid out in *Chapter 5*, *Basic Content*.

Forcing the Article type field to be mandatory

It is often a good idea to insist that certain fields are populated by making them required.

You have actually already done this in *Chapter 6*, *Structure*, when you set the relationship to the *Category* taxonomy field, but let's go through this again now.

Another typical candidate field for this might be the **Article type** field in the **Article** content type. You'll recall that its purpose is to enable us to classify Articles as either Blog posts, News, or Articles, and as such it's essential that the field is populated in order to power the various listing pages.

To set the field as mandatory, visit the **Manage fields** page for the **Article content type**, choose to edit the **Article type** field and tick the **Required field** checkbox. Then **Save settings** as shown in the following screenshot:

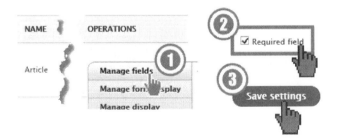

Adjusting edit form settings

Next we will look at some additional settings available for the various field types.

Placeholder text

New in the Drupal 8 core is the facility for adding placeholder text to help prompt and guide content editors. This is default text that will appear in the field before the user has typed anything in.

Let's add placeholder text to the **Tags** field to help prompt editors to fill it in properly.

Go to **Manage | Structure | Content types | Article**.

Choose **Manage form display** from the dropdown menu options, as shown in the following screenshot:

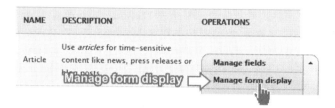

This is where you manage the various field widget settings that are active in the content-editing screens, that is, the form elements through which you interact with the field when editing content.

You are going to add some placeholder text to the **Tags** field to prompt users that they can select suggestions for words or phrases (terms) that have been used before.

Click on the cog wheel icon on the right-hand side of the **Tags** field:

You should see that the field settings area expands down to give you access to editing the placeholder text.

Enter a short prompt then click on the **Update** button:

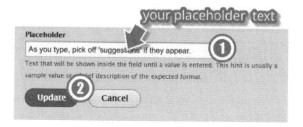

Note that after clicking on the **Update** button, you must also scroll to the bottom of the screen and click Save to make your placeholder a permanent fixture.

Once you have saved your settings, you should see your placeholder text when creating a new **Article**.

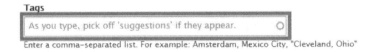

Customizing view modes

We looked at the concept of view modes in *Chapter 4, Getting Started with the UI*, but now let's look at them in a bit more detail; specifically, at how to create new ones to meet particular site requirements.

In the standard Drupal 8 install, you have two view modes active for all content types: **Default** and **Teaser**. The Teaser defines the collection of fields; their visibility and their order of display for all content when viewed as a teaser and the Default defines the presentation otherwise.

Visit the **Manage display** page again for Articles:

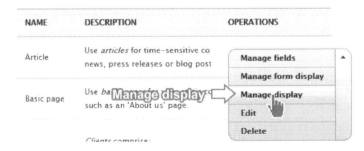

In a standard Drupal 8 installation, only RSS and Teaser view modes are customized, resulting in three secondary tabs on the **Manage display** page.

Try switching between the three tabs: Default, RSS, Teaser:

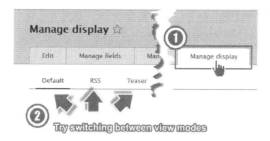

Return to the **DEFAULT** view mode and open up the **CUSTOM DISPLAY SETTINGS** region at the bottom of the page to reveal some other view modes:

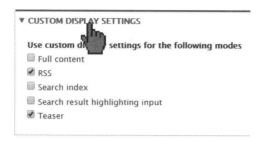

You will see a list of all view modes available for all nodes.

As you might expect, the **Teaser** view mode is already ticked since it is active in a standard Drupal 8 installation.

Ticking any one of these additional view modes tells Drupal that you wish to customize it for the particular content type—in this case Articles.

Tick the **Full content** view mode now and save the settings.

After saving the settings, you will now see an additional secondary tab entitled **Full content**. Now we can go and reshape that in terms of the fields' visibility and order.

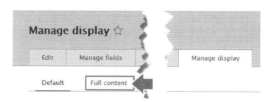

Removing the labels and fields from the display

When visiting an Article node in **Full content**, you wouldn't want to see the label on the **Category** field or to see the **Article type** field at all since the latter only exists for filtering purposes.

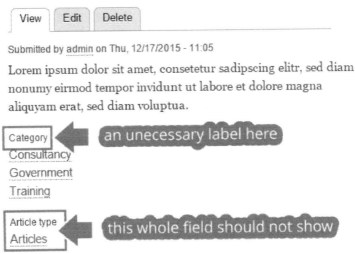

To effect these changes from the **Manage Display** page, and while this time editing the **Full content** view mode, hide the label on the **Category** field and move the entire **Article type** field into the **Disabled** area then **Save** your settings.

Controlling image size using styles

Drupal uses image styles that allow you to crop, resize, rotate and desaturate images without affecting the originally uploaded image. The default style for Articles nodes is the pre-defined **Large** which automatically scales the image to 480 x 480 pixels.

Adjust the image style from **Large** to **Medium**, and then click on **Update** and **Save**.

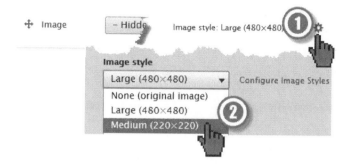

Go back and look at a full view of any Article node to see the effect which should be a re-scaled image:

Creating new content types

When we were going through the site-building scenario in *Chapter 5, Basic Content*, we defined four more content types that we need on the website: Services, Clients, Testimonials, and Frequently Asked Questions (FAQs).

We'll now work through building each of these content types and add extra fields of various types as we go.

Creating the Client content type

To create the Client content type first visit: **Manage | Structure**.

Click on **Content types** and then **+Add content type**.

Name your new content type and optionally include a brief HTML-formatted administrative description which will appear on the Add content page.

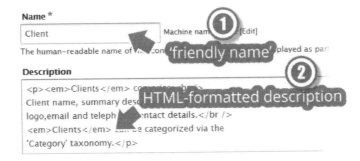

In the additional settings area at the bottom of the screen, under **Submission form settings**, change the label for the **Title** field to Client name so as to prompt your content editors to supply just that.

Note that you can provide an optional set of further guidelines and disable the **Preview before submitting** setting if you so wish.

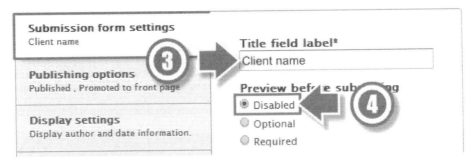

In the **Publishing options** section, untick the **Promoted to front page** option as you probably won't want Clients promoted.

Likewise, we are not interested in displaying who created Client content items so un-tick **Display author and date information** in the Display settings section.

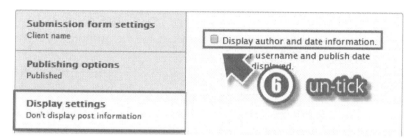

Lastly, you probably wouldn't want content editors putting individual clients into a menu and certainly not into the Main navigation menu, so un-tick all menus in the **Menu settings** section.

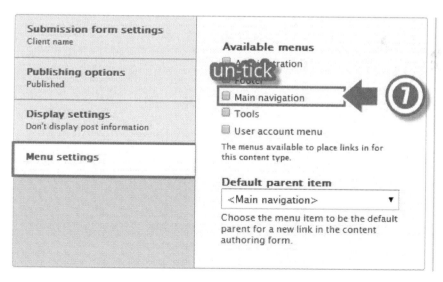

You have now created and configured the Client content type as a whole; the next step is to add some new fields, so do so now by clicking on the **Save and manage fields** button.

Inherited fields

When you are taken to the **Manage fields** page, you might be surprised to find that you have inherited an instance of the **Body** field.

Adding a logo field

Add a new **Image** type field to hold the client logo.

You may also notice a section here entitled **Re-use an existing field**. More about that will be given later. Click on the **Save and continue** button.

On the first page of options, you can leave all the default settings as they are and simply click on the **Save field settings** button.

Since the field is designated to hold logos, it might be a good idea to limit the types of images to only PNG and GIF, thereby eliminating the potential for someone uploading a low-quality JPEG.

In the following settings page, adjust the **Allowed file extensions** to be png, gif, as shown in (1) in the following screenshot:

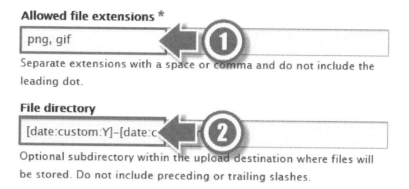

Tokens

Drupal stores images and other asset-based fields' contents as actual physical files, then references them from within the database. The **Files directory** input in the previous screenshot enables you to be specific about exactly where you want these stored on a field-by-field basis.

Notice the default use of [date:custom:Y] and [date:custom:m] in this input.

These are examples of *tokens* that get replaced in real time when used throughout Drupal. Thus, if you uploaded files on a particular day for example, 18 December 2015, these tokens will result in the uploaded logos be stored physically in the path:

```
/sites/default/files/2015-12
```

Image accessibility

For good accessibility, notice that the **Alt field** is enabled and required by default, thereby enabling content editors to attach Alt text to their uploaded logos so that, for example, users with a screen reader can interpret what an image is displaying.

Click on **Save settings** to complete this field.

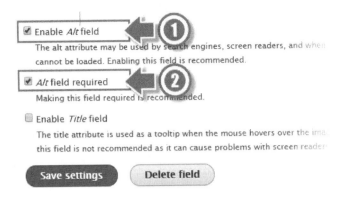

Linking clients to their web sites

It will be useful to be able to reference a client's website URL when viewing their details; you can use the core **Link** field type to achieve this. The Link field (provided by the Link module) allows you to create fields that contain internal or external URLs and optional link text.

Add a new field labeled Website and set the field type to **Link,** and then click on **Save and continue**.

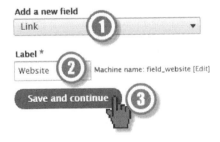

In the next screenshot, you get the opportunity to say just how many URLs you might want to add to each Client. The default of a single value seems the right choice here.

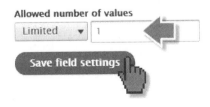

For this example, we'll set the **Allowed link type** to **External links only**, and we'll set the **Allow link text** to **Required**. Finally, we'll make the default title be `Client website`.

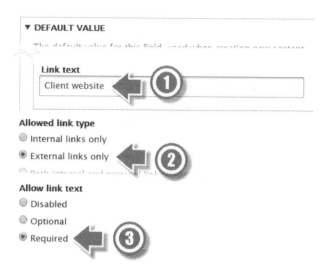

Configure your Website field as shown in the preceding screenshot and click on **Save settings**.

Providing an e-mail address for a Client

Using exactly the same procedure as in the Website field, now add a new **Email** field so that you can also provide a contact (mailto:) link for the client. In this case, the optional help text aside, you can leave all the field settings at their defaults.

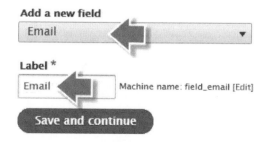

Continue with all the default settings and save the field.

Providing a telephone number for a Client

Again, using the same procedure as before, now add a new Telephone field with a field label of Telephone so that you can also provide a contact number.

Again, you can leave all the field settings at their defaults.

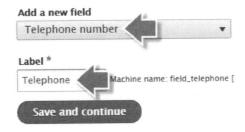

Marking a Client as high profile

Finally, in order to illustrate the use of the **Boolean** field type, add a High profile (yes/no) field to your Client content type, which you can later use to filter your list of clients down to those you wish to promote most prominently.

Leave the **Allowed number of values** to the default of 1.

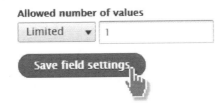

Initialize with the following settings: **"On" label** as `High profile` and **"Off" label** as `Not high profile`.

By default, the Boolean field only shows the **"On"** label value as a single checkbox.

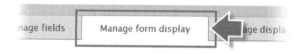

However, it's worth noting here that you have other options as to how the field is represented within the input form. You can, for example, show it as two checkboxes, which, while not really right here, might be useful in other scenarios.

To see the options, visit the **Manage form display** page again for the **High profile** field.

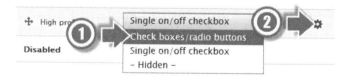

Adjust the Widget to be **Check boxes/radio buttons**.

Now when you create a Client node, you will see that the input for the **High profile** is a little more verbose.

Note that the N/A entry is there because we did not insist on the field being mandatory.

Having tried this out, it's probably best to put the setting back to the original **Single on/off checkbox** version.

Attaching taxonomy

In *Chapter 5, Basic Content,* we said that we want to be able to categorize Clients into one or more Work areas.

The easiest way to achieve this is to enable content editors to apply terms from within the **Category** taxonomy vocabulary by reusing the field that we created earlier.

Reusing fields

Visit the **Manage fields** page again and choose to **Re-use** the existing **Category** field but relabeled as Work area as follows:

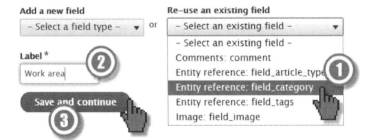

Detailed discussion of the idea of reusing fields is beyond the scope of this introductory book save to say that reusing existing fields is a good recommendation when you become a more advanced site builder. See drupal.org/node/1577260 for more.

Once you've added the field, you can optionally make it mandatory and/or choose a default value but neither of these are required for now.

Also, make sure you select only the **Category** vocabulary in the **REFRENCE TYPE** section.

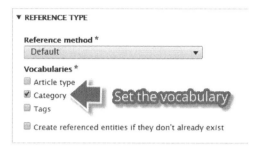

Adjust the widget on the **Manage form display** as you wish. In the following example, we have opted for Check boxes/radio buttons because there are only currently six terms in the Category vocabulary.

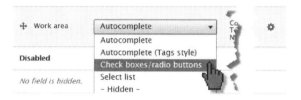

Finally, in this field-adding exercise, adjust the fields order on the **Manage form display** page so that you have the following in this order with these widget settings:

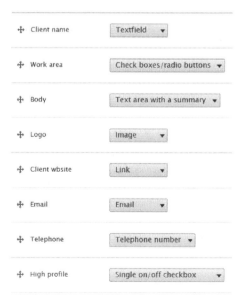

Do not concern yourself with the presence and/or relative positions of the other fields right now as these all get placed neatly into the **Secondary editing region** anyway.

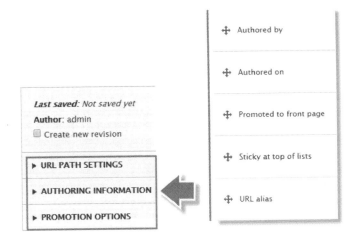

Create at least three Clients now and classify them with a mixture of Work areas.

You'll notice that the logo and contact details display at the bottom of the Full content view clearly need attention!

Adjusting field display settings

The contact details collection is easily cleaned up on the Full content view by visiting the **Manage display** tab and editing the **Default** fields and labels' visibilities as follows:

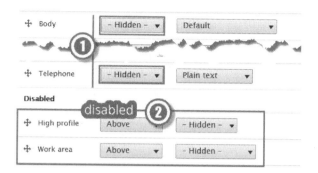

Note which fields we have chosen to disable here so that we only see the fields that we should and without unnecessary labeling:

Similarly, when viewed as a **Teaser**:

1. Trim the Body right down to a 140-character Twitter-size taster.

2. Move the **Links** so as to position the **Read more**.

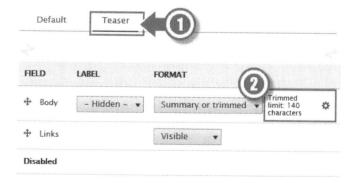

Adding a sorted client list to the Clients page

This is further revision of what you covered in *Chapter 6, Structure*, when you created a **block** using the **Views** module, this time without quite so many step-by-step illustrations.

Start by visiting **Manage | Structure | Views** then...

1. Create a new View called Clients that provides a block listing.

2. Set the **Show** setting set to **Content** and the **of type:** set to **Client**.

3. Under **BLOCK DISPLAY SETTINGS**, set **Display format** to **unformatted list** of **teasers**.

4. Visit **Manage | Structure | Block layout** and place the block, untitled, in the **Content** region but only visible on the Our Clients page (in our case, that's /node/4).

You should end up with the Our Clients page looking something like this:

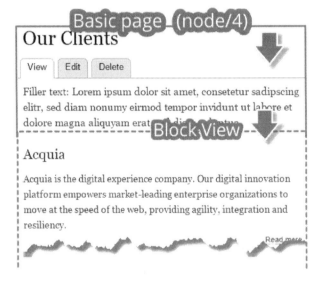

Views sort criteria

This time we'll add a little more functionality to the View as to list the clients with the high profile setting at the top.

You can edit the view directly from within the Our Clients page by using the contextual links. You'll see three sets of contextual links as you hover: one for the editing the page, another for editing the first Client, and below that, a third one for editing the View.

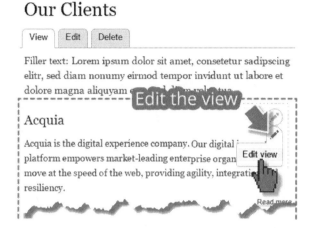

Edit the view and locate the SORT CRITERIA section at the bottom left of the screen.

Click on **Add** to add another criterion:

At first sight, the field popup dialog might seem a little overwhelming, but it is in fact a highly usable field-section/filtering tool. The idea here is to make the primary sort criteria work off the value of the **High profile** and thereby promote those clients to the top of the list.

Click in the **Search** input and type a few letters from the field name and you will see the list of fields, and so on, automatically narrow down so that you can locate the **High profile** field.

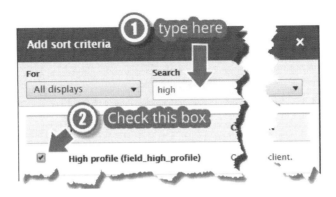

Click on the **Apply (all displays)** button to add the field as a new sort criterion.

In the following dialog, choose **Sort descending** because we want to ensure that those clients with the High profile field checked are listed first, and so sorting on that field in descending order will work.

You will see the new field added as a second sort criterion, but we need to rearrange the criteria to make the newly added one the first in the list. Click on the menu icon to the right of the list and drag to rearrange before applying the changes to all displays.

In the modal popup window, reorder the fields so that the High profile field is the first sort criteria and hit **Apply (all displays)**.

If all is well, the two sort criteria are now in the right order to do the job.

Save the view; the high profile clients should be listed first.

Adding a pager to your view

Assuming that you have quite a few clients, you won't want all of them listed all at once on the Our Clients page since that may have a performance effect in terms of page load time. Fortunately, the Views module is equipped with a **pager** facility that enables you break up your lists into sensibly sized chunks.

We'll create a pager for Our Clients view now.

Locate the central region in the View edit dialog, specifically the **PAGER** section. Note that your list is currently limited to only five items because the current setting is to **Display a specified number of items.**

In the following dialog, pick the option to use a **Page output, full pager** and apply this to all displays.

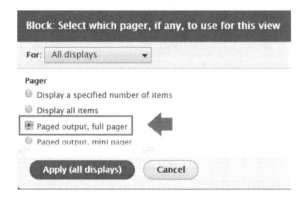

You can change the number of items on each page, but the default value of five items per page is probably a good choice. Since we only have three Client nodes right now, let's set it to just two.

Don't concern yourself with the other two options here for now.

Further down the same popup window, you can also override any of the default text labels on the controls for moving forward and backward through the various pages.

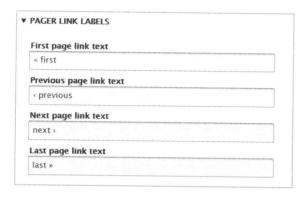

Apply the settings to all displays, save the View and you should see the pager in action.

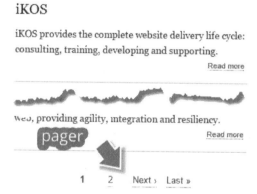

Creating the Service content type

Creating the basic Service content type and adding in the Taxonomy reference field is exactly the same as for the Client covered step by step earlier in this chapter.

To create the Service content type first visit: **Manage | Structure**, click on **Content types** and then **+Add content type**.

Repeat what you did before to create yourself a Service content type with the following basic settings:

- **Title field label**: Service
- **Preview before submitting**: Disabled
- **Published**: YES
- **Promoted to front page**: NO
- **Display author and date information**: NO
- **Available menus**: NONE

Add/adjust fields:

- Re-label the **Body** field to **Description**.
- Add a `Work area` field linking up the terms from the Category taxonomy vocab—hint: you can again reuse the existing Category field.

Click the **Save and manage** fields button.

When you're done, the **Manage fields** page should look like the following:

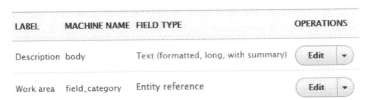

On the **Manage form display** page, set the widget to **Checkboxes / radio buttons** just as you did last time when you re-used this field. Adjust the order of the fields in the **Manage display** screen so that, in the Teaser view mode, the **Body** field is truncated to 140 characters and the Link field is moved to the bottom.

Enabling the linking of Services to Clients

It may be very useful to be able to make references to one or more Clients from within a Service so as to show the capacity in which you have worked with them.

In order to make one or more direct references from a Service node entity to a Client node entity, you'll need to use a **Reference | Content** type field.

Add a **Reference** field now labeled 'Clients'.

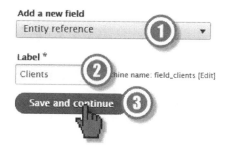

In the field settings page, set the **Allowed number of values** to Unlimited and make sure that the type of item (actually the type of entity) is set to **Content**.

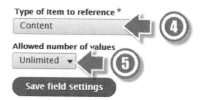

Finally, in the **REFERENCE TYPE** section, set the content type so that editors can only make references to Client entities.

Note that when creating a new Service from now on, as you type a character or so into the **Clients** field, Drupal will search through the database and offer suggestions.

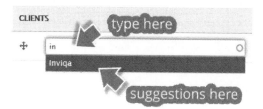

Also, since you made the field a multi-value (unlimited) one, you can add as many other clients as you like.

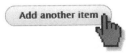

Create at least four Service nodes, each linked to at least one company.

	TITLE	CONTENT TYPE	AUTHOR	STATUS	UPDATED	▼
☐	Drupal training courses	Service	admin	Published	04/16/2015 – 12:30	
☐	Supporting your websites	Service	admin	Published	04/16/2015 – 12:29	
☐	Drupal development	Service	admin	Published	04/16/2015 – 12:27	
☐	Drupal consulting	Service	admin	Published	04/16/2015 – 12:24	

Displaying services listing using Views

As yet another revision of what you covered in *Chapter 6, Structure*, create another block view now that provides a block listing of teasers of all services in a two-column grid format. As a reminder, the quickest and easiest way to set the grid format is to choose it from within the basic Views wizard when you first opt to create the block.

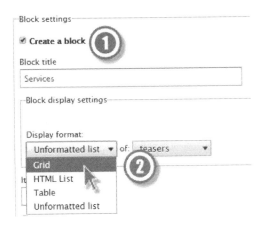

When you click on **Save and edit** to go into the Views editing screen, you can then adjust the grid setting to two columns.

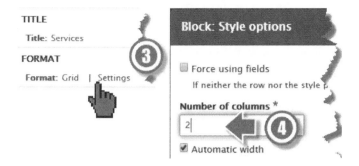

Place that block on the Services page (in our case /node/3).

Once you have adjusted the various fields display settings teaser, the finished Services page should look something like the following (shown here in a mobile view):

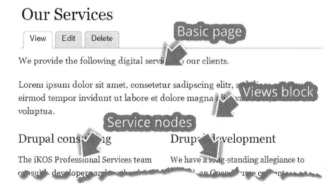

Creating the Testimonial content type

Next, create another content type to hold client testimonials, each of which holds the details (name, job role etc.) of the person providing the reference.

To create the Testimonial content type first visit: **Manage | Structure**, click on **Content types** and then **+Add content type**.

Set up the content type with the following basic settings:

- **Title field label**: Testimonial title
- **Preview before submitting**: Disabled
- **Published**: YES
- **Promoted to front page**: NO
- **Display author and date information**: NO
- **Available menus**: NONE

Add/adjust fields:

- Re-label the **Body** field to **Testimonial statement**
- Add an **Individual** plain text field to hold the testimonial writer's name.
- Add a **Role** field **(Text plain)** to describe the writer's role.
- Add a Work area field linking up the terms to a single term from the. Category taxonomy vocab' — hint: you can again reuse the Category field.

When you're done, visit the **Manage fields** page, which should look like the following:

LABEL	MACHINE NAME	FIELD TYPE
Individual	field_individual	Text (plain)
Role	field_role	Text (plain)
Testimonial statement	body	Text (formatted, long, with summary)
Work area	field_category	Entity reference

Based on all the exercises you have already done with regard to form management, the suggested field order for the (editing) form page with the Work area (Category taxonomy) widget set to Checkboxes/radio buttons might be as follows:

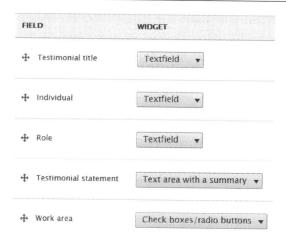

Adjust the **Manage display** (Default) settings so as to hide the unnecessary labels on the Individual and Job description fields and disable the visibility of the Work area field.

For the **Teaser** display, let's just have the Title (will always show anyway), the Individual, and the Role fields on display plus the Links for the Read more:

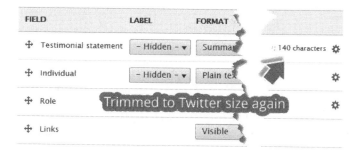

Once you have set up the new content type and added the various fields, create several testimonials, all marked as relevant to different Work areas (Category terms) and with an individual's name, role, and company name.

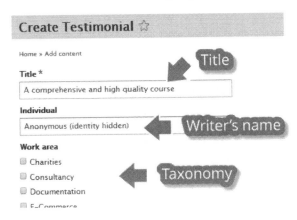

If all is well, the **Default** and **Teaser** views of a Testimonial should look like those shown below. Note you can view the teaser version on the front page if you selected **Promoted to front page** in the publishing options:

Create at least three more Testimonials now so that you have something to work within the next section.

Listing testimonials with a view

You are now going to create another view, and this time to list all your testimonials.

In the next section, you will also see just one example of the type of customizations that you effect on a view—in this case, how to group testimonials according to the Work area(s) that they relate to.

As you have already seen, the Views module is a very accessible tool for querying and presenting site content, and even the core version provides you with a range of options for providing both pre-filtered, pre-sorted, and user-filterable lists in a variety of formats.

Creating a grouped view

This view will list a number of testimonials nodes together under a heading of **E-Commerce**, another under **Consultancy** and then some more under **Training** as illustrated in the following screenshot:

This time around, we'll return to using a Page view again rather than a block because we don't have an existing Testimonials page into which to embed a block anyway.

Starting with a page view is also a good vehicle for learning how to switch a View from being a content view (based in view modes: default, teaser, and so on) into a field-based view.

Start by creating a new view in the usual way via the opening wizard screen that filters content down to just **Testimonials**.

Once you have clicked on **Save and edit** and are in the main edit screen, locate the **Content** link inside the **FORMAT** section on the left-hand side of the View edit page. This controls the style of each item in the output and defaults to **Content** with a **Display mode** of **Teaser** which should make good sense to you.

Click on the link:

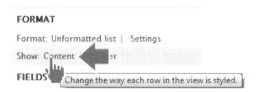

Change to **Fields**, then **Apply (all displays)**, and then, finally, **Apply** again.

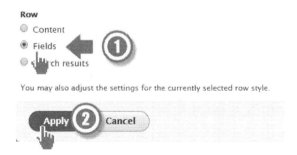

Go with the defaults settings on the next popup window and then Click on **Apply** one final time.

Opting for the Fields style means that instead of rendering each Testimonial using either the **Default** or the **Teaser View modes**, you have the opportunity to specify exactly which fields are included in addition to the Title.

You are going to add the following extra fields: Individual, Role, and Work area.

Click on the **Add** button in the **FIELDS** section.

Typing ind in the Search input should be enough to locate the **Individual** field. Check the field once you find it.

 Note that you do not need to add each field one by one, but you can enter another Search, and locate and check the next field.

Check the **Role** field.

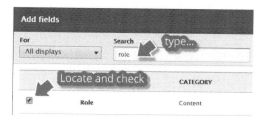

Also, check the **Work area** field.

Then, finally, click on **Apply (all displays)** again, and you will be taken through a series of dialogs asking you further questions about how you would like each field rendered in the output of the View.

If the **Individual** field was the one you added first, then that will be the first you are asked more about.

Now that you are adding fields individually, the various labels' visibility settings that you set up within the Display views modes (in Manage Display) should all be respected, but if you omitted to hide the labels, then you can do so now by simply un-checking the **Create label** field and then clicking on **Apply**.

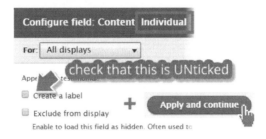

You can do the same for the **Role** field.

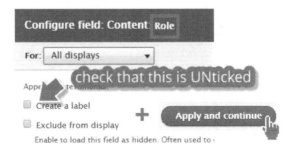

When it comes to the **Work area** field, things are different because while you don't actually want this field to be visible in the views output, the data from the field needs to be included in the view in order for the Views module to be able to group the testimonials by that field.

Thus, in this case, you should to tick **Exclude from display**.

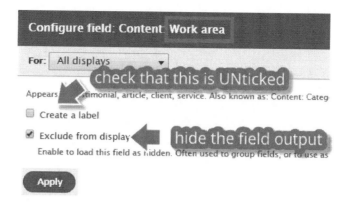

In the next window, choose to forego the link to the Taxonomy term by un-checking the **Link label to the referenced entity** checkbox.

You should then see all four fields listed in the **FIELDS** section on the left-hand side:

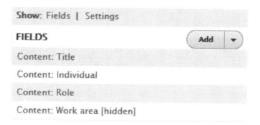

To illustrate one of the many fine-tuning options that are available within Views, click on the Fields **Settings** link in the **FORMAT** area:

Opt to present the Individual and Role fields inline separated with a spaced pipe (that is, space | space):

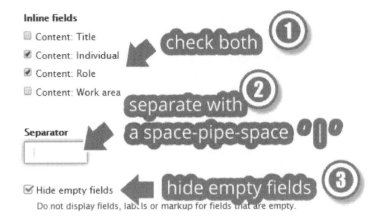

At this point, the un-grouped view should appear as shown in the following screenshot. Scrolling down the views page to the Preview area shows how the combination of putting the two fields inline and applying the **Hide empty** fields works well for us.

The final piece of the puzzle is to ask the Views module to group the testimonials by Work area so that, for example, all the Training-related ones appear listed together.

You'll remember that we opted not to display the Work area in the View earlier on, but we, nonetheless, needed the field to be present in order to perform the grouping.

Do this by adjusting the **FORMAT** settings again:

This time choosing the **Work area** field as the **Grouping field** and **Apply**.

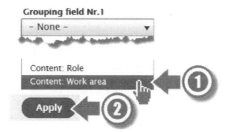

Once you have saved the view, your finished Testimonials page should appear as shown in the following screenshot.

One thing you will notice is that there is still work to be done if one or more Testimonials are tagged with more than one Work area since, with the current grouping in place, Views treats every combination as a separate group:

We could easily devote a whole chapter if not a whole book to various Views recipes using all of the core options for filtering, fine-tuning presentation, content aggregation, caching, and access control to name a few, but we'll keep things simple for now.

Finally, you'll notice that there is no **Read more** link for each testimonial. This is because we have made a field-based view, and although the titles are linked to the full content by default, you might also want to add a specific read more link as well.

To do so, edit the view again and add one of the Views module's special built-in fields, the **Link to content** field.

Save the view and you'll now see a custom **Read more** link on each testimonial.

The FAQ content type

We'll create the FAQ functionality now using only core functionality, but later in *Chapter 12, Extending Drupal*, we will extend its behavior by extending the Views module so as to improve the presentation, particularly on mobile devices.

The build for the FAQ content type is very similar to the existing three that you have already created (Client, Service, and Testimonial) with the only real differences being that we will re-label the Body field as the Answer, and we probably don't need to have a summary populated, so we can adjust the settings accordingly.

Lastly, we'll also use the FAQ functionality to demonstrate how you can build live-querying tools that empower your site visitors to interactively filter content according to their own selection criteria.

Content type settings

- **Title field label**: Question
- **Preview before submitting**: Disabled
- **Published**: NO
- **Promoted to front page**: NO
- **Display author and date information**: NO
- **Availability in menus**: NONE

It also makes good sense to re-label the Title as the word Question since this way, when presented with a list of standard Teasers, the viewer will see a list of actual Frequently Asked Questions, each of which they can click on to go through to the answer.

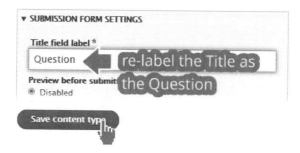

Field settings

- Re-label the **Body** as **Answer**
- Make the field mandatory
- Set the text format on the **Answer** field to be Full HTML by default because we might want to add in URLs, tables and so on for a richer answer

- Remove the facility for adding **Summary input** text to the **Body** field

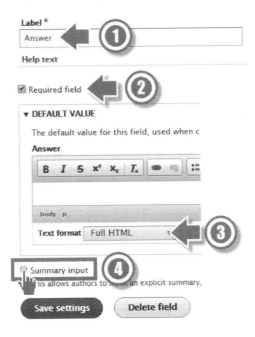

Finally, add yet another shared use of the Category field to the FAQ so that you can categorize it accordingly to a Work area: Consultancy, E-Commerce, and so on. As with all previous uses of the shared field, set the *widget* in the **Manage form display** page to **Checkboxes / radio buttons**.

Display settings

As with the last two content types, we will hide the **Links** field and the **Work area** field in the **Default** view mode.

The **Teaser** view mode should only be the **Question** itself, that is, the **Title** and the **Links** (for the **Read more**).

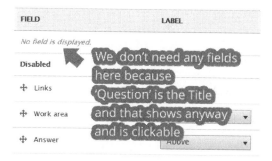

Create at least three FAQ nodes, each categorized with different Work areas such as Consultancy, e-Commerce, and Training.

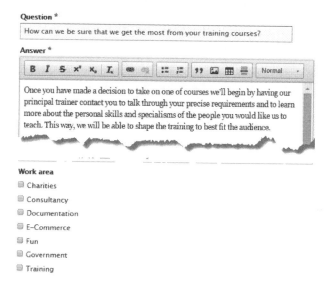

Creating the simple FAQ page

The final step is to create the actual FAQs page using the Views module as we have done earlier.

With this new view, though, we are going to take it a step further and equip the view with the ability to live-filter the results to FAQs that are tagged with particular taxonomy term(s). For example, if the user were to choose E-Commerce from a dropdown menu, then the FAQ list will be filtered down to only those marked with that Category term.

Set up a new page view that provides access to a page at /faq is also accessible from the **Main navigation** as with all the other page views that you have created.

The output from the basic view should be like the following:

Frequently Asked Questions

How can we ensure that we get the most from a training course?

If you forget to include the page view in the Main navigation menu or for any reason you need to adjust the path, it's useful to know that you can adjust these settings within the main Views editing screen in **the PAGE SETTINGS** section in the center of the UI.

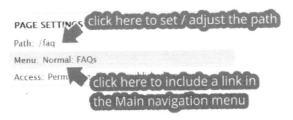

[Take care when adjusting the menu settings since Views does not necessarily default to the Main navigation menu.]

Adding interactive querying to a view

Edit your FAQ view via the contextual link toward the bottom left of the UI just above the **SORT CRITERIA** section where you can add a new filter criterion.

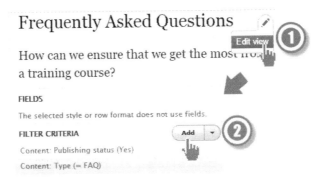

Add a new filter criterion to enable filtering via applied taxonomy terms.

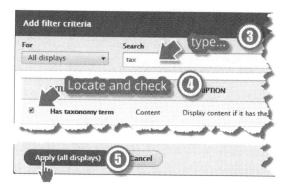

In the following dialog, choose the **Category** as the taxonomy vocabulary of interest and **Dropdown** as the widget, and then click on **Apply and continue**.

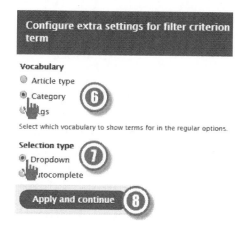

The next step is to **Expose this filter to visitors to allow them to change it** so that they can see the dropdown menu.

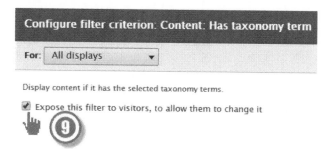

Then, directly underneath, you may wish to relabel before applying the settings.

You should now be able to the see the newly created and exposed filter in place.

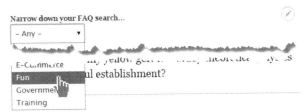

Save your view. You have empowered your visitor to live filter the FAQs page.

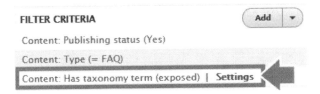

This works well, but it doesn't come with a Reset button included automatically.
To add this, go to the **Advanced** section on the right-hand side of the Views editing window and locate the **EXPOSED FORM** section, and then click on the **Settings** link.

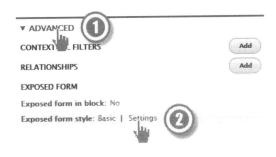

You can then adjust the text for the filter and the reset buttons.

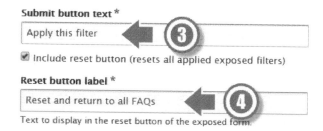

The result will be a useable client querying screen. Note, however, that our FAQs are set to be unpublished by default, so only published nodes will show.

Summary

In this chapter, we covered examples of extending existing contents in terms of extra purpose-built field types such as e-mail, link, and the entity reference type.

We looked at some alternative data-entry widgets and how the finer control options work for display output, including resizing images for optimal output.

We then looked in detail at creating four new content types and at some extra options within the standard Views UI for presenting the content in a variety of ways.

In the next chapter, we'll look at more of the configuration options that Drupal 8 has to offer, including setting up user accounts.

8
Configuration

Many of Drupal's modules include a settings screen that can be accessed from the **Configuration** menu. In this chapter, we will work our way through these screens to describe the options available and how they apply to the web site.

People – Account settings

The user account settings screen can be reached at **Configuration | People | Account settings** (`admin/config/people/accounts`).

The section is quite extensive and covers a few different areas, so we will look at them individually.

The type of website you are building will dictate the exact choices you make here, but it's important to consider all the options in turn before you allow users to start creating accounts.

Note that the actual management of users and permissions is covered in the *Chapter 9, Users and Access Control*.

The website you are building has the following requirements:

- You need individual user accounts for different people in the company.
- Visitors (anonymous users) should be able to create an account.
- Visitors should not be able to post comments.
- Site members should be able to post comments without approval.

Keep these requirements in mind as we work through the user configuration pages.

The configuration comprises multiple sections shown in the following screenshot, all collapsed to save space:

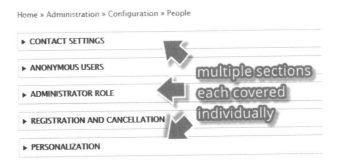

Contact settings

When a user has a personal contact form, a contact tab appears on that user's account page:

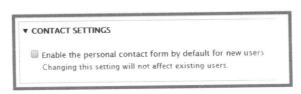

By unchecking the checkbox here, all newly created users will not have a personal contact form on their account page. You can still select it to enable one on a per-user basis; the setting here only configures the default for new users. If the setting is enabled on a particular user, other users with the permission **Use users' personal contact forms** will be able to send e-mails to them using the form.

 On a new installation, only authenticated users can use contact forms. This is a good default as it prevents spam e-mails being sent to users by web bots.

Anonymous users

If you allow anonymous users to perform any actions such as comment or create content on the website, then that content will be shown as being submitted by the Drupal username **Anonymous**. The name displayed is easily changed here to something of your choosing—a common alternative is to use the word Guest.

Change the value to Guest now.

Administrator role

When modules are enabled for the first time, they may define new permissions. It is generally convenient that your highest permission role is granted these new permissions so that users in that role are able to use and configure the module right away.

The Administrator role is the default role that is assigned the new permissions, but you can use this dropdown menu to change the role to an alternative. For example, you may have a Superuser role to which you want all new module-management permissions to be assigned automatically.

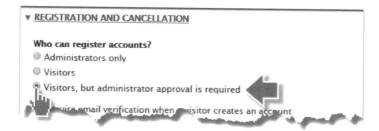

In your site, we can leave this setting as it is.

Registration and cancellation

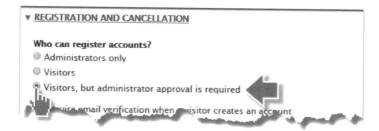

This screen allows you to define the behavior for newly created user accounts. Firstly, you can determine who is entitled to create new user accounts. The setting here is often determined by the type of site you are building:

Who can register accounts	Example uses
Administrators only	A private site or intranet.
	A site that does not have user interaction.
Visitors	A blog site where new users are encouraged to create content, an open forum, or an e-commerce site.
Visitors, but administrator approval is required	A blog where comments are moderated.

 If you select the '…administrator approval…' option, don't forget that someone will have to manually enable each newly registered user account. This can be very time consuming for a busy site.

Based on the requirements we mentioned at the beginning of this section, we will need to change the setting to **Visitors**.

We will keep the checkbox for e-mail verification ticked so that people can only create accounts if they have a valid e-mail address. This should reduce the amount of spam accounts.

Enable password strength indicator

Unchecking this box will prevent the password indicator showing on the new user creation page. While this is a useful tool to assist the user in selecting a password, some find it annoying and it might not work well on old browsers.

Account cancelation behavior

A canceled user account in Drupal does not necessarily mean that the account is deleted. The next option allows you to determine what happens to the user account itself and to the user-generated content when the user account is canceled.

For example, if a user has commented on a news article, what should happen to the comment if the user account is deleted?

The options are given in the following table:

Option	Examples of why you might use this option
Disable the account and keep its content.	You want to keep any content the user has created but do not want the user to access the site or create any more content.
	You may want to allow the user to access the site again at a later date.
	You want to preserve the threads of conversation in comments.
Disable the account and un-publish its content.	You want to keep the content the user has created but want to prevent other site users seeing it.
Delete the account and make its content belong to the Guest user.	You want to permanently remove the user account but keep the content the user generated. Any content this user generated will now be displayed as "guest" or anonymous content.

Note that it is possible to set a permission for a role to enable the user to make their own decision on what happens to their content when they delete their account.

For our example, to make sure you don't lose any content if a user account is deleted, you should use the third option otherwise when a key member of the content-editing team left, all of the content they created would be deleted.

Select **Delete the account and make its content belong to the Guest user.** Now, when a user account is deleted, the author of the article or comment will be shown as belonging to **Guest**.

Notification e-mail address

There are a number of system e-mails (discussed next) sent in response to certain user-related events.

The from address of the e-mails will default to the site e-mail address set in **Configuration | Site information**, unless you set a different value here.

For example, you might want the site e-mail to be info@mysite.com but the from address for automatic e-mails to be noreply@mysite.com.

Emails

These are the emails that are sent out automatically in different user scenarios.

They are triggered based on some of the settings you have just been looking at in the previous section.

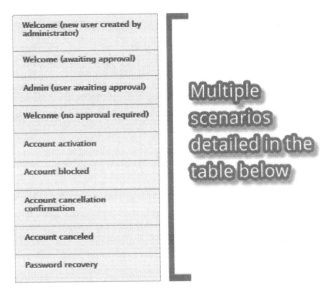

Welcome (new user created by administrator)	An introductory e-mail is sent to a new user whose account was created manually by a site admin user. This corresponds to having the new account registration setting set to Administrators only. It would also be triggered if a new user is created in the People screen even if another new account registration setting were selected.
Welcome (awaiting approval)	This is a welcome e-mail telling the user their account has been created, but they will not be able to use it until the account has been approved. This corresponds to the Visitors, but administrator approval is required for selection in new account registration settings.
Admin (user awaiting approval)	This e-mail is sent to the Notification Email Address of the site to tell you a new user is waiting for you to approve their account.
Welcome (no approval required)	An introductory e-mail is sent to a new user when there is no other account verification required.
Account activation	A notification e-mail is sent to the user when their account has been approved by a site admin and is ready for use.

Account blocked	A notification e-mail is sent to the user when the account has been blocked by a site admin informing them that their account can no longer be accessed.
Account cancellation confirmation	Confirmation e-mail is sent to the user when they request the cancellation of their account. This will contain a link to confirm the cancellation request so that the user does not cancel their account by mistake.
Account canceled	Confirmation e-mail is sent to the user after they have verified the account cancellation request and the account has been cancelled.
Password recovery	An e-mail is sent to the user in response to filling in the password reminder form. This will contain a one-time link to reset their password.

You can change the contents of any of these e-mails so that you can set the tone of voice and message to match your audience.

When you edit the templates, note the use of *tokens* here again such as [user:name].

Tokens are elements that are replaced live by actual content in the message that gets sent out. For example, the [user:name] token gets replaced by the actual username of the currently logged in user, in our case admin.

While some tokens are optional, it's important not to remove key information like the one-time login URL ([user:one-time-login-url]) on a password reminder e-mail.

Available tokens are as follows:

Token	
[site:name]	The name of the site as set in Configuration	System	Site information.
[site:url]	The full URL of the site including the prefix http://.
[user:name]	The username of the user the e-mail being sent is related to.
[user:mail]	The e-mail address of the user the e-mail being sent is related to.
[site:login-url]	A link to the login page of the site.
[site:url-brief]	The website URL.
[user:edit-url]	A link to the user profile edit page of the user the e-mail is related to.

Token	
[user:one-time-login-url]	A link that allows the user to login to the site once only without their password. This is used for password resets.
[user:cancel-url]	A link to a page allowing the user to confirm cancellation of their account.

In our scenario, the e-mails that will be active are as follows:

- Welcome (no approval required)
- Account blocked
- Account cancellation confirmation
- Account canceled
- Password recovery

If you are using Dev Desktop for your site development, you will be able to test these e-mails assuming that you used real e-mail addresses when setting up the site and user accounts.

System

The next section of the configuration page is concerned with site-wide settings. The section is broken into two subsections.

Site information

The Site information screen can be reached at **Configuration | System | Site Information** (admin/config/system/site-information).

It allows you to set some important site-wide parameters for your site.

Setting	
Site name	This setting is used throughout the Drupal site to represent your site—from the <title> tag displayed on each page to the welcome e-mails sent out to new users.
Slogan	The Slogan field is used in the default themes and is the strapline or purpose of your site.
Email address	The main e-mail address of the site—this is the address that any contact forms will be sent to by default and the default from address of any messages sent out by the site.

Setting	
Default front page	When a user visits your site domain name with no additional data in the URL, this is the page that will be presented. You can specify node/x where x is the node ID you want the user to see.
Default 403	When a user attempts to visit a page they are not permitted to see (such as an admin page when they are not logged in), they will be presented with the page entered here. You can specify node/x where x is the node ID you want the user to see.
Default 404	When a user attempts to visit a page that does not exist on the site, they will be presented with the page entered here. You can specify node/x where x is the node ID you want the user to see.

Cron

Cron is a technical term referring to timed processes that run on a webserver.

Typically, these are used for background tasks like cleaning old stale cache data and indexing search terms. Many Drupal modules will react to a cron event and perform relevant background tasks.

Depending on the purpose of your site, it may be appropriate to run cron once a day or once a minute. This choice really depends on what background tasks will run and how often they need to be triggered.

You can either run cron manually or set how often it should run automatically. The default value is every 3 hours and this is an appropriate setting if you are not sure.

The latter is a useful setting to have switched on locally when you are developing a website as it will essentially simulate a cron run every three hours. However, it may become annoying to experience the delay cron running every time you go back and visit your site after anything more than a three-hour period away so you may choose to switch it to **Never** and only run cron manually when you need to test its effect.

Cron ☆

Home » Administration » Configuration » System

Cron takes care of running periodic tasks like checking for updates and indexing content for search.

Last run: *38 min* *sec* ago.

For a live site you will need to configure your web server to call the cron task in Drupal periodically, and the setup will vary depending on where you eventually host your site. The setup is, therefore, beyond the scope of this introductory book but is detailed thoroughly at: `https://www.drupal.org/cron`

Also note that there is a link in this screen that allows you to run cron manually from outside of the site. It's deliberately a rather long URL so that people cannot guess the path.

To manually simulate a cron run simply from this screen, click on the **Run cron** button.

Content authoring

The settings within this section control the experience of content editing for your users. It's quite a complex area with many options, so we'll go through one step at a time.

Text formats and editors

Go to **Configuration** | **Text formatters and editors** (`admin/config/content/formats`).

You will see four text formats listed, the particular JavaScript editor that is assigned to them, and which roles can use them:

NAME	TEXT EDITOR	ROLES
✛ Basic HTML	CKEditor	Authenticated user, Administra...
✛ Restricted HTML	—	Anonymous user, Administrat...
✛ Full HTML	CKEditor	Administrator
✛ Plain text	—	*This format is shown when ...*

CKEditor is the name of the WYSIWYG editor included with Drupal 8.

We first looked at fields back in *Chapters 3, Basic concepts*, and *Chapter 4, Getting Started with the UI*. You also touched on the idea of text formats back in *Chapter 5, Basic Content* when you first looked at creating and editing page content, specifically the **Body** field, which is a text area rather than simply a single line of text.

Text formats apply whenever there is a text area field in use. It is possible to specify a text formatter on a per-field basis.

The idea of text formatters is that different markup effects can be applied in different scenarios. For example, you may not want people adding links in article comments.

In normal use, the text formats are allocated to a site role (see roles and permissions in *Chapter 9, Users and Access Control*). Thus, some users can use advanced formatting while others may only have more restricted options.

Let's explore this by looking at the **Basic HTML** format. Click on the **Configure** button on the **Basic HTML** row.

We can decide which roles are permitted to use this text format. You'll see from the checkboxes that this formatter can be accessed by users when they are logged in to the site.

 Note that there is also a dropdown menu that suggests that you can choose from a variety of JavaScript editors in addition to the **CKEditor**. However, by default, there are no other editors installed.

You'll recall how, back in *Chapter 5, Basic Content*, we were able to demonstrate how the toolbar changes when you switch between Basic HTML and Full HTML.

You can configure the toolbar that is available to the user when editing text areas in this particular text format.

Try dragging some buttons from the available list to the active toolbar now. You'd most likely want to do this if the type of content you are creating calls for addition HTML elements, for example, superscript or subscript if you are creating mathematical content.

As a rule, we want to keep the Basic HTML format simple so that it is easy for all content editors to understand.

Further down the page, we have the **CKEditor** plugin settings. It is configured so that you can include images within text areas and those images will be automatically uploaded to Drupal.

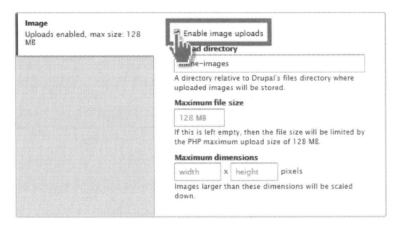

 Not everyone likes this function as it is very easy to break the layout of a page by uploading an image of an inappropriate size directly into an HTML area. We recommend using image fields instead wherever practical, like the one you saw in *Chapter 5, Basic Content* when you created your first Article.

If you don't want to allow images to be uploaded to text area fields that are using this format, untick the **Enable image uploads** box.

Note that dragging away the image button also removes the plugin:

In general, adding or removing elements from the toolbar will also adjust the corresponding plugins and their respective settings.

The final three sections of the screen (**Enabled filters, Filter processing order,** and **Filter settings**) work in combination.

There are a number of filters that can be set to automatically apply. The filters are actually applied at the time of building the page and do not modify the original content. We'll go through in detail what each one of these does, but you'll see here that you can easily enable and disable the filters using the checkboxes.

Underneath the filter list, you'll see that some filters have a settings panel and the order in which filters are applied can be changed by dragging them up and down the list.

Depending on what you are looking to achieve, the order in which the enabled filters are applied could be important.

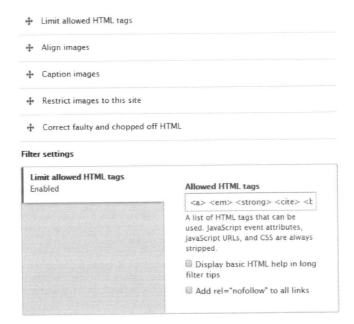

Available filters

Name	Description
Limit allowed HTML tags	Strips out any HTML in the content except for those tags included in this list. Note that you can specify which HTML tags you want to allow in the settings for this filter.
Display any HTML as plain text	Do not allow any HTML markup at all—strip these out completely and only display as plain text.
Convert line breaks into HTML	When the user has entered line breaks and paragraph breaks in the editor, convert these to ` ` and `<p>` tags so that the same layout is achieved in a web browser.
Convert URLs into links	If a URL is entered in the text, automatically make this a link so that the user doesn't have to when creating the content.
Align images	This applies an HTML 5 standard attribute to image tags to correctly align them.

Name	Description
Caption images	This applies an HTML 5 standard attribute for image captions.
Restrict images to this site	This ensures that images used are hosted within the same domain so that you cannot reference images on an external source.
Correct faulty and chopped off HTML	If the user has entered html directly, attempt to correct any mistakes or missing tags.
Track images uploaded via a Text Editor	This ensures that images uploaded via the editor are displayed correctly if they are updated elsewhere in Drupal for example, by editing the image in the files tab under: Manage | Content | Files (`admin/content/files`)

Don't forget to save your settings after making alterations.

User interface

The user interface section allows you to define some settings for the back end/admin behavior of Drupal.

Shortcuts

Shortcuts appear in the top menu, and when clicked on, show a second level of navigation. If there are a common set of tasks you use to manage your Drupal site, it may be useful to add them here.

You have been using the shortcuts throughout this book so far in the form of the links for **Add content** and **All content**.

You can set up multiple shortcut sets and assign them to different users. This allows you to set up easy navigation for different types of users of your site without exposing them to the full range of settings, which may be confusing.

Let's improve the default shortcut set now on our site at:

Configuration | User interface | Shortcuts (admin/config/user-interface/shortcut).

Press the **List links** button and you will see the three existing ones; two defaults and the Status report on you added back in *Chapter 4, Getting Started with the UI*.

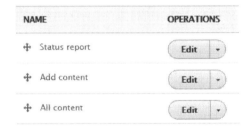

We'll add two new shortcuts now using different techniques. Firstly, we'll add a shortcut to the permissions page, which will be useful in the next chapter.

Click on **Add shortcut**.

All we have to do now is give the link a name (Permissions) and then add the path: /admin/people/permissions.

Click on **Save** and rearrange the order so that they now appear like this:

We'll add another shortcut second in a different way like you did back in back in *Chapter 4, Getting Started with the UI.*

Go to **Content | Comments** and click on the star symbol next to the **Comments** title:

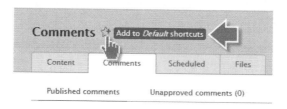

Go to **Configuration | User Interface | Shortcuts** (admin/config/user-interface/shortcut).

Your shortcuts set should now contain four links in total.

Note that you can change the order as before by returning to the listing page and dragging and dropping the list items.

Development

The development section has a number of screens and settings that are most useful when you are building your website and less so once it is live. The settings here are often different between development and going into production. Some of these settings will be changed just before a site goes into production.

Performance

The performance settings page has two subsections that perform distinctly different functions.

Caching

For anonymous visitors to your website, it's very common for each visit to a specific page to return the same generated HTML.

Depending on the complexity of the page, Drupal will have to make many calls to the database to collect all of the data it needs to assemble the page view. If the page is always the same, it is wasted effort to reassemble it every time someone requests the page. Therefore, we can specify that the generated page output is cached for a certain period of time.

This means that subsequent visitors to the same page will receive it more quickly and with less effort by the web server.

The downside of caching is that if you change the content, the user may be presented with the cached page and not see the updated content. This is why you can set the maximum age of the cache here to anything from no cache at all to 1 day. A good compromise is about 3 hours, but you must make sure that you have a non-zero value specified here or your site will be very slow.

There has been a great deal of work in Drupal 8 to develop internal caching so that it is cleared in an intelligent way when content is updated. This means that if you do change something in an article for example, it will be cleared in the cache even if you have a long cache lifetime value.

Clear cache

Once you have spent any amount of time working with Drupal or looking online for answers to common problems, you will inevitably come across the response: "Have you cleared the caches?"

There are many sets of data Drupal needs to process a page that are called every time. It is not very efficient for these to be loaded from the source database each time. For this reason, these data are cached for varying lengths of time. Often you will find that a change to a setting will not be immediately obvious on the website. This is a common scenario where the cache is delivering the data and the website does not know about the change yet.

Pressing the **Clear all caches** button on this page will reset these caches and force Drupal to reload the latest values, rebuilding the cache at it does so.

Note that when you do click on this, the next page and any other pages will be slower the first time they load after clearing cache as Drupal rebuilds its cache data.

Bandwidth optimization

Drupal modules often introduce their own CSS and JavaScript files to support module functionality. As there are often a large number of modules enabled on a site, this can lead to many small files being delivered per page request. This means that a web browser has to make multiple requests to load the page and therefore increase the total time for the page to load. In addition, some older web browsers will only load a certain number of JS and CSS files before stopping—meaning that pages on your website will not render correctly.

To avoid this problem, Drupal is able to aggregate the JS and CSS files, that is, join all those small files together and deliver them in one request (or at least a significantly smaller number of requests).

Note that both **Aggregate CSS files** and **Aggregate JavaScript files** are enabled by default.

Logging and errors

When working on a site, various modules will log errors and warnings in different scenarios.

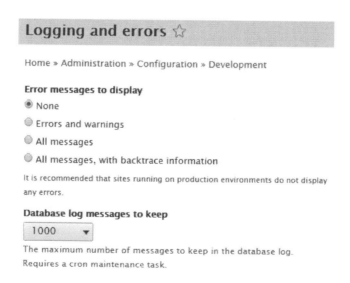

The first section determines whether error messages are displayed on the screen in the messages region of the page. This is useful when you are building a site but should always be set to **None** when your site is in production mode—otherwise your users could see some rather ugly error messages that they probably cannot do anything about.

In the second section, the **Database log messages to keep** value determines how much data is stored in the `watchdog` database table; this is the table where logging messages are stored and can be viewed at **Reports | Recent log messages** (`admin/reports/dblog`).

This database table will keep growing infinitely as the site is used, so it's a good idea to keep just the most recent messages.

We'll be looking in more details at reports later.

Maintenance mode

If you are working on some changes to your site that might cause problems for users, it can be useful to place the site to **Maintenance mode** while you perform the work. This means that only users with the permission **Use the site in maintenance mode** can view anything on the site.

This permission would usually only be applied to administrator level users:

For everyone else, you can customize the message that is displayed to the user:

Note that **@site** will be replaced with the site name set at **Configuration | Site information** (`admin/config/system/site-information`).

Configuration synchronization

Detailed coverage of configuration management is beyond the scope of this beginners' book but in short, this section empowers you to export either the entire configuration of your site; content types, taxonomies, views and so on as a single (zipped) archive or to choose to target one particular item such as a view to be exported as pure code.

It also enables you re-import and even provides a neat comparison view of what's changed in your configuration since you last exported it.

This section is enormously useful when it comes to deploying new or updated configuration from a development site to live.

Media

Next we will look at the different settings available for media management in Drupal 8.

Go to the **Configuration** page where you will see a number of entries under the heading **MEDIA**.

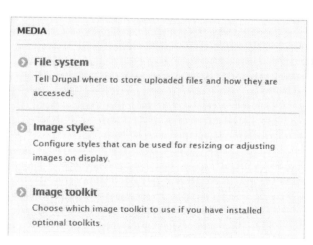

File system

Starting from the top, click on the **File system** option.

Later we will find that other modules give us more options in this screen, but for now, let's have a look at what this setting screen tells us.

Public file system path

sites/drupal-8.dd/files

A local file system path where public files will be stored. This directory must exist and be writable by Drupal. This directory must be relative to the Drupal installation directory and be accessible over the web. This must be changed in settings.php

The public file system path is the location on the web server where any files uploaded to Drupal via the user interface will be placed.

The public file system folder can be found inside the `sites/default/files` folder in your Local Drupal codebase.

You can locate the Drupal codebase on your computer now using Dev Desktop; click on the **Local code** link on the control panel:

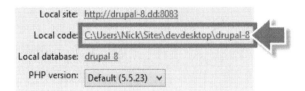

Then navigate down to public files folder at `sites/default/files`.

The **Temporary directory** is used when files are uploaded for temporary storage. The value of this depends on the operating system your computer or server is running.

It is important to note that Drupal understands what files are available based on a database table that is updated when files are uploaded. For this reason, simply copying files to the folder will not allow them to be used within Drupal.

This is also where the **Delete orphaned files after** setting comes in.

Delete orphaned files after

Orphaned files are not referenced from any content but remain in the file system and may appear in administrative listings. **Warning**: If enabled, orphaned files will be permanently deleted and may not be recoverable.

If a file exists in the folder but is not in the Drupal database, it is considered orphaned and will be cleaned up periodically. The length of time between becoming orphaned and the file actually being deleted is set here. You'll not normally need to adjust this.

Image styles

We looked at image styles earlier when we were applying them to content fields in the section entitled *Customizing the display*, back in *Chapter 4, Getting Started with the UI*.

You may recall, by default we have three image styles:

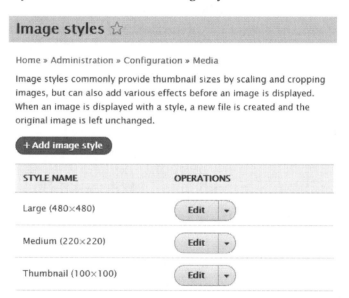

You can modify these from their default settings or we can define completely new ones.

To recap, image styles are used to apply to images uploaded as content on your website. This means that even if your users upload huge photo direct from their camera, Drupal can automatically resize the image so that it is appropriate for use on the Web.

Also, this functionality means that we don't need to manually create lots of different size versions of an image for use as thumbnails. This is all completely automated using image styles.

We can also apply more advanced image styling such as color desaturation, as we'll see next. This means you can apply consistent effects for images across your site without having to remember something like the Photoshop filter settings used.

Let's go back to our scenario now and create a new image style.

Click on **Add image style** and create a new style called `Black and white thumbnail`.

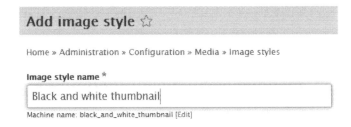

Click on **Create new style** and you will be on the image style editing screen, as shown in the following:

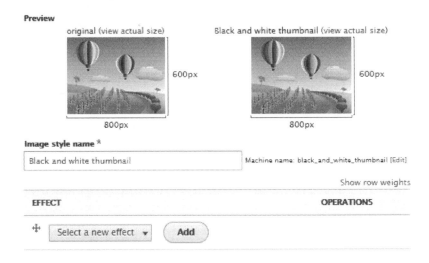

Image styles are created by applying a number of image effects one after another. Once all the image effects are applied, Drupal saves a modified copy of the image, leaving the original one untouched. This means that when the styled version of the image is required, it is quickly available.

Click the **Select a new effect** dropdown and you'll see there are a number of different effects.

Each of these effects can have additional settings as well, as described in the following:

Effect	Description
Convert	This converts the original image format to a new format— PNG, JPG, or GIF. This is useful if the original images are uploaded in a format that is not commonly used in web browsers.
Crop	This allows you to crop the image to a preset size. This means that parts of the image outside of the crop size will be lost in the styled version. You can also specify where the center of the crop should be.
Desaturate	This removes all color from an image (converting it to black and white) and offers no further options.
Resize	This allows you to specify the exact size of the styled image. Note however this can cause the image to be distorted if (for example) you enter square dimensions for an image that was originally rectangular.
Rotate	This rotates the source image by a specified angle. You can also specify the background color that is exposed as a result.
Scale	This is similar to resize but the aspect ratio (shape) of the original image is retained. This avoids the distortion effect you can end up with when using resize. When dealing with images, it's always better to scale down rather than up for best quality. For this reason, this option will only allow scaling more than 100 percent of the original size when specifically set to do so using the Allow Upscaling option.
Scale and crop	As you might have guessed, Scale and Crop is a combination of the scale and crop actions where the image is scaled to the smaller dimension specified with the larger one being cropped. This is a way to make a square thumbnail out of a rectangular image without distorting the image.

For our scenario, we are going to replace our image thumbnail style for the Article listing to be a desaturated square.

Press **Select new effect** and then select **Scale and crop** and press **Add**, set the width and height to 200 and click on **Add effect**.

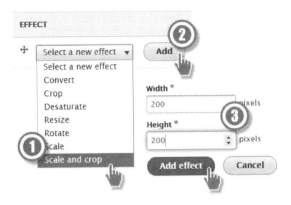

You'll now see that the list of effects for your style has been updated:

Press **Select a new effect** again and this time choose **Desaturate**.

You should notice that when you return to the style page, you will see a preview of the image style with the effects applied.

Each time you apply a new effect, you will see the preview update.

Be sure to press **Update style** when you have everything as you want.

Now we have created our new style, which we can apply to the Article content type. To do so, visit **Structure | Content types** (`admin/structure/types`).

Locate the **Article** content type (**1**) and click on **Manage display** (**2**) on the article content type dropdown.

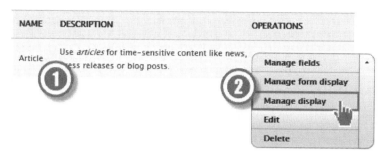

You'll recall that back in *Chapter 7, Advanced Content,* you customized the `Full content` view mode for the Article content type so to see the effect of your new Image style in action, switch to the **Full content** view mode in order to apply it.

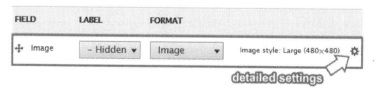

Locate the image field and click on the gear icon.

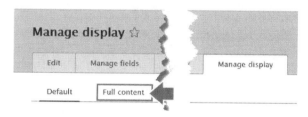

Now change the image style from **Large** to **Black and white thumbnail**.

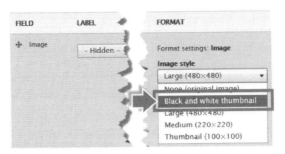

Click on **Update** and then take care to also hit **Save,** and when you go back to the news page that you made on the site in the *Working with the Views module* section in *Chapter 6, Structure,* you should now see that the new image style has taken effect, as shown in the following:

Image toolkit

A final note about image resizing before we move on.

Go back to the **Configuration** page and navigate down to the **MEDIA** section again.

The setting here determines the quality of JPEG images when they are resized. The default value is 75 percent, which is a reasonable compromise between file size and quality.

However, we'll change the value to 90 percent so as to have slightly better quality resized images.

Before we do, try drastically changing the quality to something like 10 percent so that you can see the effect of JPEG data loss, and then the save the configuration settings and go back to the news page to see the effect.

Search and metadata

As we add more content to our demo site, it might be useful for us to add a search function for our users. Drupal 8 has a built-in search that we can configure here.

Go to the Configuration page again and look at the contents of the **SEARCH AND METADATA** section.

Click on **Search pages** and you will see the configuration for the main search of the site.

We'll work our way through these settings now.

Indexing progress

In order to allow users to search for content, Drupal will index the content in its search database. When new content is added to the site, this is not indexed immediately but is instead queued to be processed later. This shows you how many items of content have been indexed and how many are waiting.

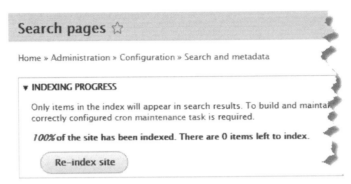

Note that if you choose to re-index the site then you will also need to run cron again manually to update the index.

Indexing throttle

Drupal will look at the contents of the indexing queue periodically in what's referred to as a Cron task, as discussed earlier in the chapter in the *Cron* section. This basically means the indexing process will happen in the background periodically. We'll discuss how to set this up later, but for now we should assume this will be running once every 3 hours.

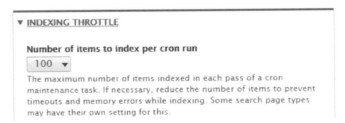

If lots of content is created, we can add a throttle so as not to overwhelm the webserver by trying to process all of the content at once.

Instead, we can set a throttle so that (as is the default) only 100 items are processed each time.

This is a sensible default for most sites.

Default indexing settings

The default indexing settings allow you to have more control over what content is added to the search index.

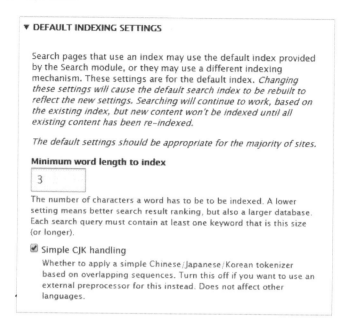

By default, only words of three characters or more are indexed, but you can change this if you want. This default is sensible though as there's not much value in searching for two letter words in most sites.

Logging

By default, searches are not logged.

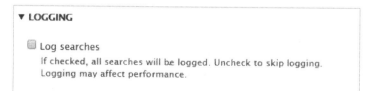

If you change this option, every search carried out will be recorded to the Drupal database. This can have a negative effect on performance, so it is usually sensible to leave it switched off.

Search pages

The last section of the search configuration page is the most important one.

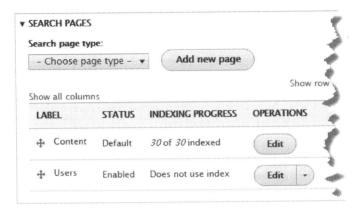

Before we go into detail here, click on the **Back to site** link to go back to the site and see how the search works now.

The search box appears on the left-hand side of the screen.

Let's try out an example search now based in the content we added earlier.
Try searching for dog.

Notice the search term used is highlighted in the results.

At the top of the screen, you should see two tabs. These tabs represent the different search pages as detailed in the configuration screen we were looking at earlier.

Search for dog

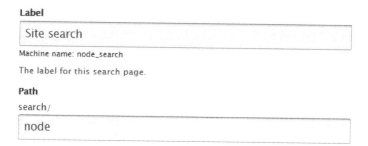

If you switch between the tabs, you are searching different types of content for the same search term.

Go back to the search configuration now **Configuration | Search pages** (`admin/config/search/pages`).

We will look in more detail at the search page configuration for content.

Select **Edit** next to the **Content** search page.

Here we can control a number of things about the search page.

The **Label** corresponds to the value in the tab the user can see.

Let's change this to `Site search`.

The path is the URL of the search page—we can change this as well, but for now let's leave it alone.

Label

Site search

Machine name: node_search

The label for this search page.

Path

search/

node

Finally, we can change the content ranking settings, which determine the order of the search results. If a user searches for a term that is commonly used in the content across the site, it can be useful to change the influence of certain factors so that more relevant content appears earlier in the search results.

Changing the settings as follows would mean that more recent content that is promoted to the front page will appear earlier in the rankings.

Don't forget to save the changes.

FACTOR	INFLUENCE
Number of comments	0
Keyword relevance	0
Content is sticky at top of lists	0
Content is promoted to the front page	5
Recently created	10

This is easier to see in effect when you have lots of content on the site, but have a play with these settings now and see how they change the searches you perform.

 Note that you can also create multiple search pages with different influencing factors if you want to create a more complex search on your site.

URL Aliases

Now go back to **Configuration | URL Aliases** (`admin/config/search/path`) (inside the **Search and metadata** section).

When you create content in Drupal, it is assigned a unique node ID (referred to as a `nid`).

You can use this to view the node on your site by entering the URL as follows:

`/node/nid` for example, to view node 1, the URL is `/node/1`

Rather than having to know the `nid` of all content, you can also specify one or more URL alias entries that will also get you to the page.

For example, `/latest-news` is easier to remember than `node/55`.

You can also use URL aliases for promotional URLs, for example, `/competition` linking to `node/1234`.

The URL alias page shows a list of all aliases that have been created.

At the moment, this is blank as we have not been setting up aliases for our scenario so far. So let's set some up now.

From the URL alias page, we can create them directly. You may remember from earlier that our **Contact Us** page is node 6.

Click on **Add alias**.

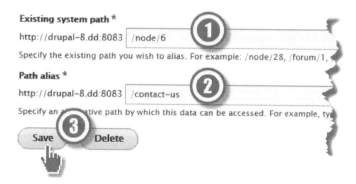

Enter node/6 for the existing system path and contact-us for the path alias. Press **Save**.

Now, when you go to the URL http://drupal-8.dd:8083/contact-us, you will get exactly the same page as if you had typed http://drupal-8.dd:8083/node/6.

Go to the page now and click on **Edit**.

If you expand the URL alias section in the right-hand side of the edit form, you should see your alias presented.

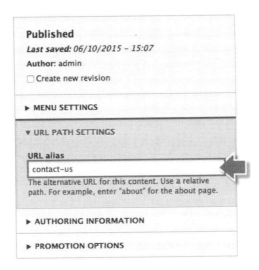

 You can have multiple URL aliases that point to the same page, but be aware that search engines such as Google could interpret this as duplicate content and penalize you as a result.

Regional and language

Drupal 8 is capable of supporting sites in multiple languages. The details of the translation mechanism are discussed later. The regional and language settings allow you to set some defaults for the target market of your site.

Regional settings

Go to **Configuration** | **Regional and language** | **Regional settings** (`admin/config/regional/settings`).

Locale

From here you can set the **Default country** and **First day of the week**. These will have been set based on your choices during the install process, but you can change them now if they are incorrect.

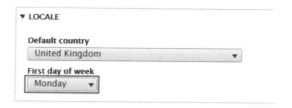

Time zones

The default time zone for the site will also have been set based on the country you selected during the install process. You can change this now, but also you can decide whether you want to allow visitors to your site to specify their own time zone.

If you allow visitors to determine their own time zone, time-sensitive data will be presented to that user in their own localized time. This would affect, for example, the posting times of articles or the time of an event.

▼ TIME ZONES

Default time zone
Europe/London

Date and time formats

Go to **Configuration | Regional and Language | Date and time formats** (`admin/config/regional/date-time`).

NAME	PATTERN
Default long date	Saturday, December 19, 2015 – 10:25
Default medium date	Sat, 12/19/2015 – 10:25
Default short date	12/19/2015 – 10:25
Fallback date format	Sat, 12/19/2015 – 10:25
HTML Date	2015-12-19
HTML Datetime	2015-12-19T10:25:47+0000
HTML Month	2015-12
HTML Time	10:25:47
HTML Week	2015-W51
HTML Year	2015
HTML Yearless date	12-19

Here you can set the date formats for your site.

By default, there will be a set of date formats which may not be appropriate for your local users:

Format Name	Presented as
Long	Saturday, December 19, 2015 - 10:23
Medium	Sat, 12/19/2015 - 10:23
Short	12/19/2015 - 10:23

For example, in the UK, dates are presented as dd/mm/yyyy as opposed to mm/dd/yyyy, so let's change this now.

Click on **Edit** on the **medium** date format and edit it to the UK standard.

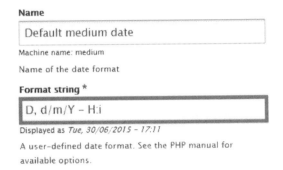

Entering a valid date format string here will ensure that all dates presented in short form will display in your new format. You can see the effect of this immediately in the preview.

Similarly, edit the **short** format to UK style too.

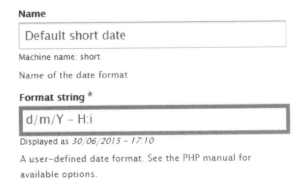

The current value uses standard PHP abbreviations for dates that can be found in full at http://php.net/manual/function.date.php.

Now when you go back to the article list views we created earlier, the new date formats will be applied.

Web services

In the final section of the configuration screen we will look at is the web services section. In the standard installation, this relates only to RSS publishing of content on the site.

RSS publishing

RSS stands for **Really Simple Syndication** and is a standard way to share your content to people as a channel.

Precisely what you see when you enter this URL in your web browser will vary depending on your computer and browser.

In the standard installation, Drupal will expose an RSS feed of content that is currently promoted to the front page on the URL http://drupal-8.dd:8083/rss.xml.

It will be interpreted as a list of links and summaries of the articles on your website.

For example, in Google Chrome without any dedicated plugins, you will see:

```
<?xml version="1.0" encoding="utf-8" ?>
<rss version="2.0" xml:base="http://drupal-
8.dd:8083/rss.xml"
xmlns:dc="http://purl.org/dc/elements/1.1/"
xmlns:content="http://purl.org/rss/1.0/modules/cont
ent/" xmlns:foaf="http://xmlns.com/foaf/0.1/"
xmlns:og="http://ogp.me/ns#"
xmlns:rdfs="http://www.w3.org/2000/01/rdf-schema#"
xmlns:schema="http://schema.org/"
xmlns:sioc="http://rdfs.org/sioc/ns#"
xmlns:sioct="http://rdfs.org/sioc/types#"
xmlns:skos="http://www.w3.org/2004/02/skos/core#"
xmlns:xsd="http://www.w3.org/2001/XMLSchema#">
  <channel>
    <title>My Drupal agency</title>
    <link>http://drupal-8.dd:8083/rss.xml</link>
    <description></description>
    <language>en</language>

    <item>
    <title>The company pet</title>
    <link>http://drupal-8.dd:8083/blog-posts/2015-
06/company-pet</link>
    <description><span data-quickedit-field-
id="node/8/title/en/rss" class="field field-node--
title field-name-title field-type-string field-
label-hidden">The company pet</span>
<span data-quickedit-field-id="node/8/uid/en/rss"
class="field field-node--uid field-name-uid field-
type-entity-reference field-label-hidden"><a
title="View user profile." href="/users/admin"
lang="" about="/users/admin" typeof="schema:Person"
property="schema:name" datatype=""
class="username">admin</a></span>
<span data-quickedit-field-
```

By contrast, in standard Firefox, you might see:

The configuration page allows us to determine how many articles are in the RSS feed and whether you should include summary content as well as the article title.

Summary

We covered a great deal in this chapter. You saw that many modules in the standard installation profile expose a configuration screen and this controls the behavior and user interaction of the website.

In particular, we looked in detail at the e-mails sent by Drupal and more in depth image styles. As you activate more optional modules, you'll find that more configuration options become available in this section.

Next we'll look into User accounts and the detailed roles and permissions options that Drupal offers.

9

Users and Access Control

In this chapter, we will look at how Drupal uses the idea of roles as containers to allocate permissions to the actual site users. We'll investigate how to create user accounts in your example site and how you can give those users different capabilities using the roles and permission system. We will end by showing you how to customize the user management screen.

Users and roles

Drupal allows an unlimited number of **user accounts**—site users each with a unique username, e-mail address, and password—and it employs roles to which you can attach permissions. A site user's capabilities are dictated by the role(s) the user is a member of and the permissions that are assigned to those role(s).

Each role, including the special **Anonymous** and **Authenticated user** roles, is granted one or more named permissions allowing them to perform certain tasks.

A list of the currently defined roles is found by navigating to **People | Roles** (admin/people/roles):

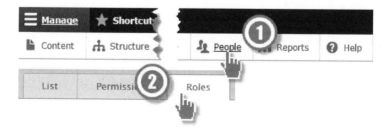

Here, you'll see a list of the roles available on your site by default:

Let's see how these roles are defined:

- **Anonymous user**: This is anyone who is not logged in, that is, public visitors to your site
- **Authenticated user**: This is used for logged in users
- **Administrator**: This is a special Drupal role that is granted a high level of permission—often dangerously high for many users and really only meant for senior site administrators

Permissions

Navigate to **People** | **Permissions** (`admin/people/permissions`).

This page lists out all the permissions organized by a module and provides a column for each role. You can see that it's possible to allocate permissions in a very granular way—a key feature of Drupal:

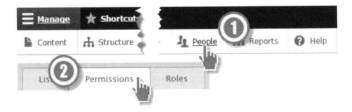

Navigate your way through the permissions grid and locate the section containing all the permissions related to the `Contact` module:

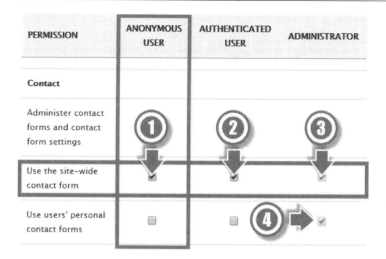

If you want both visitors and existing account holders to be able to use the contact form, then you need to allocate the **Use the site-wide contact form** permission to the **Anonymous user** (marked as (**1**) in the preceding screenshot) and the **Authenticated user** (**2**).

Note that the **Administrator** role is automatically granted all available permissions whenever a module is enabled that defines permissions, so the check box is automatically ticked (**3**).

Next, move down to the **Node** module section.

Drupal is frugal with its allocation of permissions. For example, while the Node module allows both the Anonymous user and the Authenticated user to view published content, it is very specific about who can create and edit content:

Typical roles

You are going to add three new roles, which are somewhere in-between the Authenticated user and the overly powerful Administrator in terms of authority:

- `Contributor`: This role can contribute content to the site, but it has limited content administration rights
- `Editor`: This role can also contribute content to the site, but has the administration rights over all content so that they can moderate others' work
- `User manager`: This role can only create and manage user accounts

Navigate to **People | Roles** (`admin/people/roles`) again, and add the `Contributor` role now:

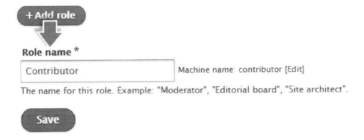

Repeat the process twice until you have three roles set up: Contributor, Editor, and User manager.

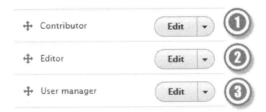

Let's look at an example scenario that we have been given, relating to various roles on our site. We'll then visit the permissions grid again and implement these stories.

A typical scenario

Let's imagine the following three criteria:

- `Contributors` should to be able to create, edit, and delete their own Articles
- The creation and editing of Basic pages is reserved for `Editors` only
- We also want `Editors` to be able to edit any content irrespective of what type of content it is or who created it

Putting aside **Revision** permissions, here are the permissions with respect to Articles:

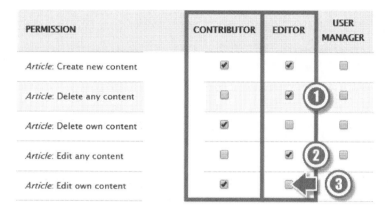

Note that we omitted permissions concerned with `Revisions` in the preceding screenshot just for clarity.

The permissions are identical for clients, services, and the testimonials sections of the permission grid, so set them up too.

In addition:

- Only the editor can delete any Articles
- Only the editor can edit any Articles
- If a role is granted permission to edit any, then editing their own is implied

Basic pages on the other hand are different, we only want editors to be able to create, edit, and delete (any of) them, so the permissions are set accordingly:

PERMISSION	CONTRIBUTOR	EDITOR	USER MANAGER
Basic page: Create new content	☐	☑	☐
Basic page: Delete any content	☐	☑	☐
Basic page: Delete own content	☐	☐	☐
Basic page: Edit any content	☐	☑	☐
Basic page: Edit own content	☐	☐	☐
Basic page: Revert revisions Role requires permission *view revisions* and *edit rights* for nodes in question, or *administer nodes.*	☐	☐	☐
Basic page: View revisions	☐	☐	☐

Once again, since editors are granted permission to edit any, then editing their own is implied.

Note that we are not assuming that editors need to be able to view and manipulate revisions—this being out of the scope of our stories.

Finally, we want user managers to manage user accounts but not more than that:

PERMISSION	CONTRIBUTOR	EDITOR	USER MANAGER
Administer permissions *Warning: Give to trusted roles only; this permission has security implications.*	☐	☐	☑
Administer users *Warning: Give to trusted roles only; this permission has security implications.* Manage all user accounts. This includes editing all user information, changes of e-mail addresses and passwords, issuing e-mails to users and blocking and deleting user accounts.	☐	☐	☑

Creating user accounts

You are going to create three new users and assign each of them to one of the new roles, so navigate to **People** and click on the **Add user** button.

Enter each user account with a unique e-mail address, a username, and a reasonably secure password.

Ensure that the account is active and you add the user to the appropriate role(s):

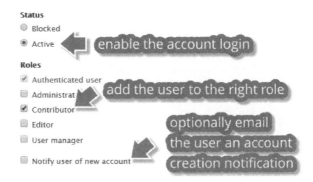

Add an optional picture to your user:

Finally, choose whether or not you would like the user to be contactable by other users. Then, go ahead and create the account:

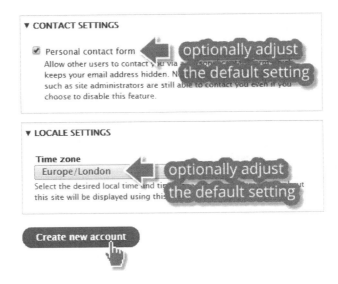

You will be notified that the account has been created:

You will remain on the same page ready to create another account.

Repeat the same procedure for creating the `Editor` and the `User manager` accounts until you have a total of four accounts.

Drupal does not allow you to use the same email address twice, but you can, for example, add a plus sign (+) into the email address and anything else to the right of that will be ignored. This works for Google mail (Gmail) and some other mail systems, so you can actually create multiple Drupal accounts essentially linked to the same e-mail address such as YourEmail@example.com, YourEmail+1@example.com, YourEmail+2@example.com, YourEmail+3@example.com, and so on, while keeping Drupal happy.

When you have created all three new accounts, visit admin/people again and you should see them listed. Take a moment to see if your user list matches this:

USERNAME	ROLES	OPERATIONS
User manager	• User manager	Edit
Editor	• Editor	Edit
Contributor	• Contributor	Edit
admin	• Administrator	Edit

Hovering over an account **Edit** link will reveal the full path in your browser status line:

For example, the User manager role, as the fourth user to be created has User ID (UID) of 4, thus the edit link is:

http://drupal-8.dd:8083/user/4/edit?destination=/admin/people.

The ?destination= suffix merely brings you back to this page after an edit. Note that destination suffixes like this are used throughout the whole of Drupal, not just on the user editing pages.

User ID 1

You are currently logged in as the administrative user with a User ID of 1.

The user with ID of 1 is a very special, all-powerful user whose actions are not governed at all by the permissions. This means that you can do absolutely anything you like without being controlled in any way by the permissions system.

Thus, even though earlier in the chapter when setting up the Contributor user account, you may have chosen not to enable the **Personal contact form**:

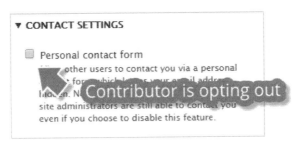

As the admin user, permissions such as these are irrelevant, so you still see the **Contact** tab:

 Once again, a very important point, as the 'admin' user, you are not subject to any form of permission control.

Editing accounts

Visit the account management page again by navigating to **Manage** | **People** (admin/people) to see the list of users.

You have already seen that you can click on the **Edit** link to edit the account details but it's worth noting too that you can also perform some account management tasks enmasse.

As an example, let's temporarily block several users from logging in.

First, select the three user accounts that you just made:

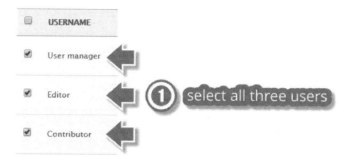

Then from the **With selection** menu, choose the **Block the selected user(s)** option and click the **Apply** button:

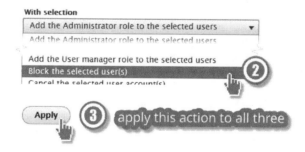

Since this is a quickly and easily undoable action, no confirmation is asked for and you will see a notification of the action and, as you can see in the following screenshot, the three users' accounts will be blocked:

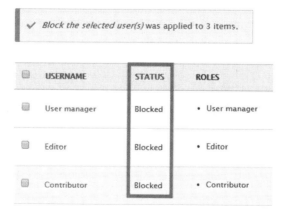

You can, and should, reactivate the accounts by following the same procedure, but this time choosing unblock:

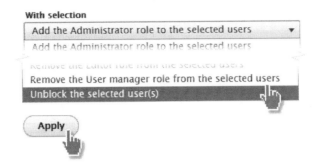

Taking control of the People page

You should note that the **People** screen, like many administrative screens in Drupal 8 is actually a `View`.

Despite the fact that you can't see the contextual links in the form of the cog wheel, you can always go the main Views listing page at **Structure** | **Views** (admin/structure/views).

Edit the view just as you would any other:

Since many of the Drupal administrative pages are also views, you can start to appreciate how easily you can modify the **People** page and many other administrative UI elements within Drupal:

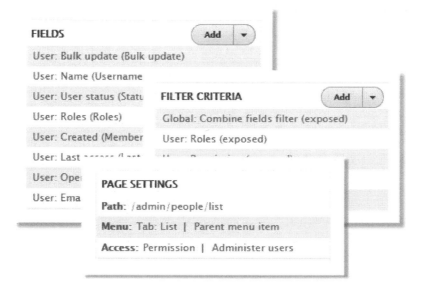

Summary

This chapter introduces just the basics of managing user accounts. We covered creating new roles and how to apply permissions to these roles with fine granularity.

It also introduces you to a fantastically powerful idea that many of the administrative UI screens within Drupal 8 -- for example the People page -- are themselves simply views, thus empowering you to take total control of the backend experience for your content-editing team.

In *Chapter 10, Optional Features*, we'll look at all of the other modules provided in Drupal 8 core that are not enabled in the Standard installation profile.

10
Optional Features

There are many features of Drupal that are switched off in the standard installation. This chapter explains what they are and how you can use them.

We will be looking at the following modules:

- Activity Tracker
- Aggregator
- Ban
- Book
- Forum
- Responsive image
- Statistics
- Syslog
- Telephone

When you visit the `Modules` page of your Drupal installation at admin/modules or from the main menu by clicking on **Extend**, you will note that a number of modules are unticked, indicating they are not enabled. Some of these modules are really meant for module developers and are outside the scope of this book, so we won't cover every single one.

Go to **Extend** (`admin/modules`) now.

Activity Tracker

The `Activity Tracker` module provides a new tab on the user account page.

Clicking on the **Activity** tab gives a list of content that this user has modified recently.

It also adds a Recent content menu item into the Tools menu block:

Aggregator

The `Aggregator` module allows you to collect information from external sources and publish it on your website. This could include RSS, RDF, or Atom feeds. For example, if you wanted to publish a list of headlines and article summaries from an external news site, you could use the `Aggregator` module.

Navigate to **Extend** (`admin/modules`) now and enable the `Aggregator` module.

Once enabled, the module provides new screens for us to manage external site feeds. You'll find the configuration page listed under the **WEB SERVICES** section of the administrative configuration page at: **Configuration** (`admin/config`):

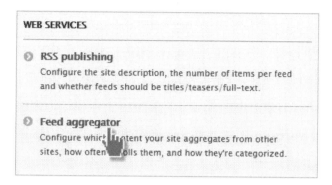

You will be taken to the overall Feed overview page where existing feeds are listed and you can add new ones.

As an example, we can set up a headline feed from the BBC news website, which provides an RSS feed at `http://feeds.bbci.co.uk/news/rss.xml?edition=uk`.

Click on **Add feed** and fill in the following details:

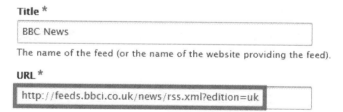

Save the new feed, and you will see a confirmation message that the feed has been created. You will be taken back to the **Add feed** page ready to add another.

If at this point you click on the **Sources** link in the breadcrumb.

You will be taken to a page listing all the current aggregator sources, of which you will find only one:

Click on the **More** link, and you will see that the Aggregator reports that it has never been checked.

The feed has not been checked and is therefore empty because the `Aggregator` module only gets triggered to check for new content on a **cron** run.

You have two options here: either run cron as described back in *Chapter 8, Configuration*, or visit the feeds overview page again by navigating to **Configuration | Services | Aggregator** (`admin/config/services/aggregator`).

Locate the BBC News feed you just set up.

Open up the menu in the rightmost **OPERATIONS** column and click on the **Update items** button:

You should then see that the number of items is set.

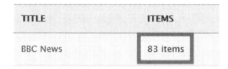

 Note that the Aggregator module will also try to update your feed every hour, but that the cron is set by default to run every 3 hours. If you really want to update your feed every hour, then set cron to run once per hour too.

The Aggregator module provides a dedicated block for each feed that you create. We'll add the **BBC News** block to the **Sidebar second** now. Navigate to **Structure | Block layout** (admin/structure/block).

Press the **Place block** button in the Sidebar second to place the new feed's output there:

Choose the **Aggregator feed** block:

You can then title the block **(1)** and choose the precise feed **(2)** to show from the select list. There is of course only one item present at the moment—**BBC News**—because you have only created one feed:

When you save the block, it will appear on all pages on your site in the second sidebar:

There is another screen provided by the Aggregator module by navigating to **Manage | Configuration | Web Services | Feed aggregator** (admin/config/ services/aggregator).

Click on the **Settings** tab to see the details:

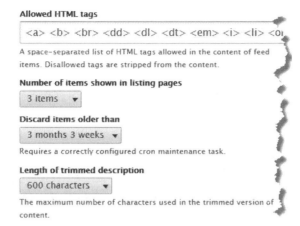

Here, you can filter some of the content from the external feed and also decide how long to retain it—bearing in mind if you take a feed from a busy site, like in our example, it won't be long before you have thousands of content items on your site.

Ban

This module allows you to block visitors to your site that originate from a specific IP address. The IP address can uniquely identify a particular user, but more commonly, it will resolve to a geographical or organizational group, such as a particular business or institution. Typically, you would want to do this if you are experiencing trouble from automated "bots", which are attempting to break in to the site or send spam via a web form.

Enable the Ban module now.

Once enabled, the Ban module provides a new configuration screen labeled IP address bans.

Visit that screen now by navigating to **Home** | **Administration** | **Configuration** | **People**

(admin/config/people/ban):

To identify potential IP addresses to ban, go to the recent log messages by navigating to **Reports** | **Recent log messages** (admin/reports/dblog).

If you see a message that reads something like **Login attempt failed from 100.200.300.400**, you can identify that a failed login has occurred from the IP address 100.200.300.400.

Note that a single failed login may not justify a ban, but if you see repeat offenders in the logs or multiple failed login attempts from the same source, you might want to copy that IP address and add it to the ban list.

Don't worry about banning yourself because the Ban module will not let you ban your own IP address.

Book

If you want to create a set of structured content rather than unrelated single pages, you can enable the Book module. This is ideal when creating a user guide where each page links to the next and content may be formed into chapters.

Enable the Book module now.

When you enable the Book module, a new content type Book page becomes available on the **Add content** screen.

As an example of how to use this module, let's digress a little from the *My Drupal agency* site build for a moment, and look at how this chapter could be created as a Drupal book.

To start with, we will create a new Book page called Learning Drupal 8. From the **Add content** screen, click on **Book page**.

On the right-hand side, there is a new expandable section, **BOOK OUTLINE**.

When you expand this item, you can add a new page to a specific place in the book structure. As this is the first book page we are creating, we can select **Create a new book**, fill in the **Title** field with Learning Drupal 8, and then **Save and publish** the page as normal:

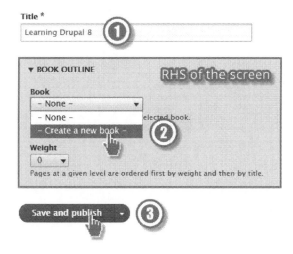

This will make more sense once you have created a few more items to go in the book.

To demonstrate, you'll now add a `Chapter 10` book page and a series of child pages as follows:

- Chapter 10 (parent)
    ◦ Activity Tracker (child)
    ◦ Aggregator (child)
    ◦ Ban (child)
    ◦ Book (child)

These pages represent the sections of this chapter so far.

Begin adding the `Chapter 10` page to the book by selecting the existing **Learning Drupal 8** book as follows. Navigate to **Add content | Book page**:

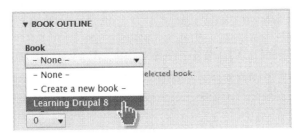

Now create each of the other pages, this time expanding the **BOOK OUTLINE** menu and setting (1) the **Book** to **Learning Drupal 8** and (2) the **Parent item** as **Chapter 10**:

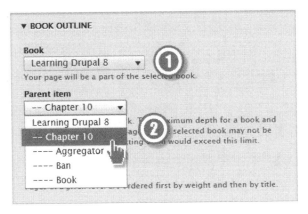

Note that you can also use the **Weight** option to change the precise order of the pages in the outline, but probably more easily done later using some dragging and dropping once the `Book` is built.

Once you have created the book pages, you can browse to the Book (`Learning Drupal 8`) from the **Content overview** page by navigating to **Content** (`admin/content`):

From here, you can now see an automatic link created to **Chapter 10** and all the other book pages:

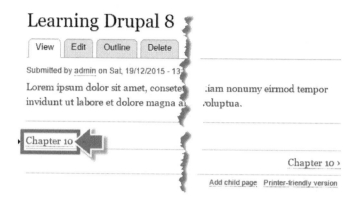

When you click through to this, you'll see links to the subsection pages that you created earlier:

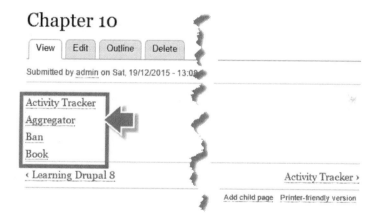

The Book module creates all of the navigation for you based on the outline choices you make.

In addition, the Book module provides extra links at the footer of each page:

- **Back**
- **Forward**

- An option to **Add child page**
- An option to present a **Printer-friendly version**:

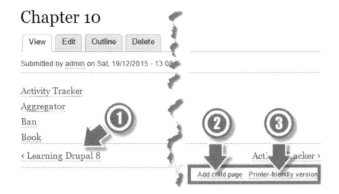

Note that the Book module adds a new tab to every item of content thus enabling you to quickly and easily include that content in any existing book or create a new book on-the-fly.

Forum

The Forum module empowers you to create discussion forums on your website.

Enable the Forum module now, and once you have enabled, navigate to **Structure | Forums** (admin/structure/forum).

When installed for the first time, the Forum module creates an initial forum called General discussion:

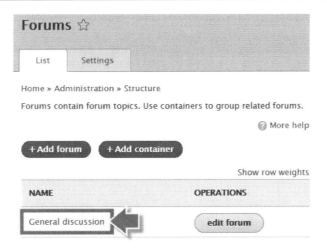

Containers

You can set up the hierarchy of your forum by creating one or more `containers` and then creating a number of forums inside these containers.

Click on the **Add container** button to create a new container:

Then, give the container a name and some optional descriptive text. After doing this, **Save** it:

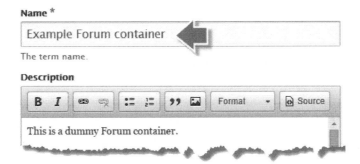

What you have actually done here is set up a taxonomy as discussed back in *Chapter 6, Structure*.

If you navigate to **Manage | Structure | Taxonomy** (`admin/structure/taxonomy`), you will see a vocabulary called `Forum`.

Click to list the terms:

Top level categories in this vocabulary represent the `Containers` and second level categories represent the **Forums**.

You can drag and drop to set up your `Forum` structure just as you like indenting to represent hierarchy:

Forum settings

Once you have set up the basic structure of your forum, you can go to the **Settings** page and change some of the behavior by visiting **Manage | Structure | Forums** (`admin/structure/forum`).

Click on the **Settings** tab:

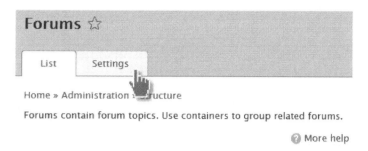

This section comprises of three settings, each one discussed here:

Hot topics

Every time someone posts a reply to a forum topic, a score is added to the topic and the hot topic threshold is used to decide how many posts are required before a topic can be considered popular (or hot):

Once a topic is marked as hot, it can be sorted to display at the beginning of topic lists.

Topics per page

Where there are multiple replies to a topic, set how many should be visible before the pager is displayed:

Default order

Most forums sort content by date, showing the newest content first. However, you can also take advantage of the hot topic threshold set here using the most active sort order:

Default order

◉ Date – newest first

◯ Date – oldest first

◯ Posts – most active first

◯ Posts – least active first

Default display order for topics.

Forum permissions

Next, you should decide who has permission to post forum topics or replies on your website. The `Forum` module exposes a number of new permissions for you to apply to one or more roles. For example, let's assume you only want logged in users to be able to post forum topics and replies.

From the main menu, navigate to **Manage | People | Permissions** (`admin/people/ permissions`).

Scroll down to the `Node` module section, to locate the settings for the **Forum topic** content type.

As you can see, only the site **Administrator** role will be allowed to create new `Forum` content initially:

Allow authenticated user to create and delete their own topics only as follows:

Remember to scroll right down to the bottom of the page and press **Save permissions** to save your settings. We'll leave Forum editing and the ability to delete anyone's forum as the reserve of (say) the Editor role.

Contributing Forum topics

To add a new Forum topic, visit the **Forums** page at: /forum and click the **Add a new Forum topic** button:

Add a new topic to the `General discussion` forum:

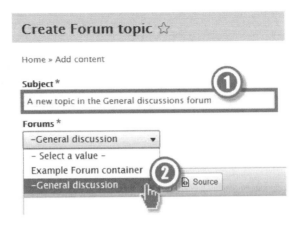

You can set the details of the content created on the right-hand side just like for any other type of content such as the ability to post the `Topic` into a particular `Book`—a very useful inclusion. However, in this case, you can leave them all set to their defaults.

Click **Save and publish** to publish your topic within the forum. Now, users with the appropriate permissions will be able to see your forum post and add comments to it:

The Forum module depends on the Comment module—a sensible idea since there is no point in re-inventing the wheel when we already have a perfectly good system for enabling threaded conversations.

 Both Forum topics and Comments can have fields added to them just like other content in Drupal. So the Forum functionality can be greatly extended, the default configuration is only a simple implementation to get you started.

Responsive image

Modern web designs need to take into account the device that is being used to view the content that Drupal is presenting. Different devices have different form factors from mobile phones, to tables, to traditional desktop computers. You may have heard of the terms 'Responsive design' or 'Adaptive design', and basically these mean that rather than having a different mobile version of your site for a mobile device, the content display is modified automatically depending on the device being used.

The following are examples of how content may be presented differently:

- Show smaller images on a mobile device to conserve mobile data bandwidth.
- Rearrange template regions to best present the most important information on a small screen size.

Responsive design relies on a concept known as a **breakpoint**. This can be thought of as the width of the screen in pixels where the design changes to a layout more appropriate for that device.

In the default theme Bartik, there are three breakpoints defined (which is a common starting point in responsive design)–mobile, narrow, and wide. You could also think of these as mobile, tablet portrait, and desktop.

The Responsive image module allows you to add some simple mobile optimization to your website.

Enable the Responsive image module now.

When activated, a new configuration screen will be available on the **Configuration** page.

Locate the **MEDIA** section and click on **Responsive image styles**:

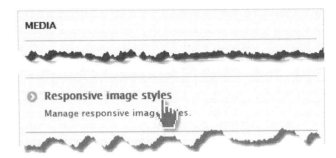

You will see two pre-defined responsive image styles:

We won't go into detail here on how to create and configure new responsive styles because that would involve too lengthy a discussion involving technical responsive design terminology.

You've already got the two pre-defined ones: **Narrow** and **Wide** so instead we'll simply employ those to kick in for your **Article** content type at the existing breakpoints.

Go to the **Manage** display page of the **Article** content type by navigating to:

Structure | Content Types | Article | Manage display (admin/structure/types/manage/article/display).

Note again that since we opted to customize the **Full content** view mode:

When you select the **FORMAT** of the **Image** field, you will see there are now a two additional ones: **Responsive image** option. Select this option:

Once you have selected this, click on the gear icon to choose the required **Responsive image** for use within this view mode:

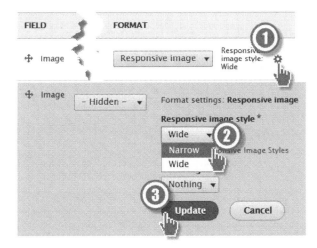

 If you use some quite distinct image styles it should be easier to spot the difference between the three breakpoints by resizing your browser window. Just bear in mind that only up-to-date browsers support this feature.

Statistics

The `Statistics` module allows you to collect data about the visitors to your site. When the module is active, the number of times each piece of content is viewed is counted.

Enable the `Statistics` module now, and you will see a configuration screen available by navigating to **Configuration | System | Statistics** (`admin/config/system/statistics`):

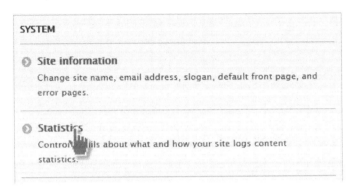

Enable the collection of stats by ticking the **Count content views** option:

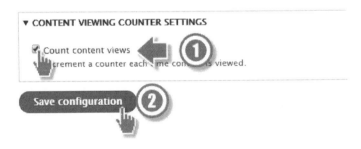

You'll then have access to a new block, which is initially entitled `Popular content`.

Visit **Manage | Structure | Block layout** and place the block.

Click on the **Place block** button now:

Choose to place the **Popular content** block.

This block can be configured to show a list of content that is:

- Most popular for the current day
- Most popular for all time (since the module was enabled)
- Most recently viewed

There are multiple sets of options available in this screen, but we'll only set the **Number of day's top views to display** for now, and we'll place the block in the Sidebar second region:

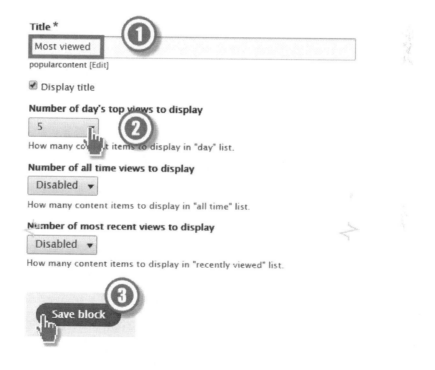

Don't forget that multiple instances of blocks can be placed within regions each with different settings.

Note that the very nature of the Statistics module requires a record to be added to the database whenever a page is viewed. Therefore, it is not recommended to run this module on a very busy website since it will have a negative effect on caching.

Syslog

The standard Drupal 8 installation enables a module called `Database logging`.

The `Database logging` module records log entries that are created by different modules and can be viewed at **Reports | Recent log entries** (`admin/reports/dblog`).

However, this means that data is written to the database, so often the database logging module is turned off in production websites for performance reasons.

The `Syslog` module is an alternative logging module, which logs the same data to the system log of the operating system Drupal is running in.

This is considered to be a faster operation than a database write and therefore is preferable for production sites.

You can alter the settings of the `Syslog` module by navigating to **Configuration | Development | Logging and errors** (`admin/config/development/logging`).

When this module is activated, Drupal's log messages will appear in the main system log on your server. You can specify log labels and patterns to help you filter Drupal messages from other content in your log files.

Core (experimental), Multilingual, and Web services

There are three sections we haven't discussed yet. These are a set of modules grouped under Core (experimental) and other sets grouped under the heading Multilingual and Web services. These are powerful sets of functionality that warrant in-depth study and there are other *Packt Publishing* titles dedicated to these topics.

Summary

In this chapter, we explored some (but not all) of the functions in Drupal core that are not enabled during the *Standard installation*. These are areas that may not be needed for every site, but are worthy of exploring and understanding.

You now know how to use the built-in Forum capabilities and how to aggregate content from another site.

Drupal core is deliberately lean in its functionality — attempting to only include the most common website functionality. The power of Drupal 8 is that you can extend this functionality with modules from the community or those you create yourself. We will explore extending Drupal further in *Chapter 12, Extending Drupal*.

In *Chapter 11, Reports*, we'll complete our journey through the main sections of the Drupal 8 administration interface looking at the Reports section.

11
Reports

Drupal 8 has a number of reporting features that you can use to find out more about what's happening behind the scenes. In this chapter, we will look into all of the reporting options available in the Drupal 8 core and how they can help you as you develop your site.

In particular, we will look at the reports enabled in the standard installation profile:

- Recent log messages
- Field list
- Status report
- Top "access denied" errors
- Top "page not found" errors
- Top search phrases
- Views plugins

Accessing reports

Click on **Manage** to expand the drawer as normal, and then select the **Reports** link:

You will then be presented with a list of the available reports on a single screen:

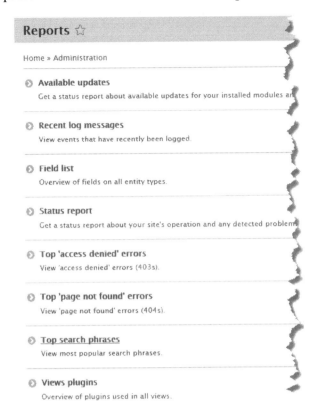

Available updates

The Update Manager module checks all installed modules against drupal.org to see if there are any updated versions available. You should see that everything is up to date as expected.

Recent log messages

The **Recent log messages** report is probably the most commonly used of the reports available in Drupal core. Any module is able to report its activity here in a standardized way, whether it is for error reporting or simply informational details.

Click on the **Recent log messages** link, and you'll see a report similar to this:

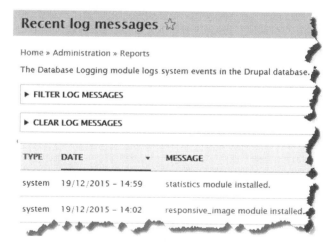

Due to the fact that any module can insert messages here, the display can be a little confusing. Each log entry has the following fields:

- **Type**: This is defined by the module that recorded the log entry and is most often the module name.

- **Date**: The date and precise time (not shown in the preceding screenshot to save space) of the recorded log entry.

- **Message**: This field displays more detailed information associated with the log entry. This can be a truncated summary, and if you click on the message, you can often get more information.

- **User**: If the message was generated from a logged in session, in which the user was logged in, this will show the user's name. If there was no user logged in, this will say anonymous.

- **Operations**: Some log messages may provide additional actions that can be carried out as a consequence of the message — this is determined by the modules, but can include, for example, a link to a settings page to fix a reported error.

Log details

Sometimes, there is more detail to a log entry than the summary report is able to display. Clicking on the message opens up another page with more log details:

Details ☆	
Home » Administration » Reports » Recent log messages	
Type	system
Date	Saturday, December 19, 2015 – 14:59
User	admin
Location	http://drupal-8.dd:8083/admin/modules
Referrer	http://drupal-8.dd:8083/admin/modules
Message	*statistics* module installed.

This provides the following additional information that was not on the summary page:

- **Location**: The URL being loaded when the log was generated
- **Referrer**: The URL immediately preceding the location URL
- **Message**: This may be a more detailed message than was presented on the summary screen
- **Severity**: The predefined severity levels are in descending order of urgency—**Emergency**, **Alert**, **Critical**, **Error**, **Warning**, **Notice**, **Info**, and **Debug**
- **Hostname**: The IP address or domain name of the user originating the request

Filtering log messages

When you have a number of modules operating on your Drupal site, it can be difficult to find the messages in the report that you are looking for. On the reports page, there is a filter system to help with this:

- Go back to the **Recent log messages** page.
- Expand the **FILTER LOG MESSAGES** section:

This will allow you to only show messages for a specific type (for example, just for one module) and specific severity. This is a quick way to reduce the number of entries, so you are only presented with what you are looking for.

For example, to check for login attempts, select **user** from the **Type** menu, **Notice** from the **Severity** list then click the **Filter** button:

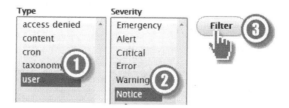

The resultant filtered report may be as follows:

This will show you only the log records of interest. Click on the **Reset** button at any time to clear the filter and display the full list.

Clearing logs

Each log message is stored in the Drupal database, up to a limit defined in the site configuration. It is unwise to store all messages forever, due to the potential amount of data and therefore database size. 1000 messages is a sensible default.

To clear the current list, go back to the main reports screen by navigating to **Manage | Reports | Recent log messages**.

Expand the **CLEAR LOG MESSAGES** section:

This has one simple function — **Clear log messages** — which will permanently delete all log messages from the database. By default, the maximum number of messages is set to 1,000; to change the setting go to:

Manage | Configuration | Development | Logging and errors:

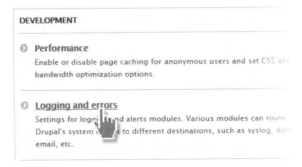

Log messages and performance

Recording so much data to your database can have an impact on the performance of your site as it gets busier. For this reason, there is an alternative module in Drupal 8 core called `Syslog`. Once enabled, `Syslog` will record exactly the same information that we have been looking at so far into the server log files rather than the Drupal database. This is a significantly faster process, if slightly less convenient for you to access as the site administrator.

Field list

The **Field list** report is a useful check on the content types you created for your site.

Navigate to **Manage | Reports | Field list**.

In the first tab, **Entities** (shown in the preceding screenshot), you can see all of the fields that have been defined for your entity types so far and which entities are using each field (in the case where a field is shared).

The second tab, **Used in views**, shows a list of fields that have been used in views that are defined on your site.

Clicking the link on the view name takes you directly to the edit screen for the view.

Status report

The status report page provides information about the settings of your site.

Navigate to **Manage | Reports | Status report**.

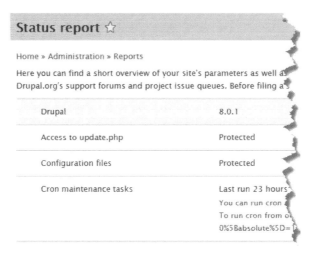

Drupal core and each community-contributed module, used on your website, can show notifications and warnings about its settings on this page.

When there is an advisory message such as the need for a security update, there will usually be instructions about how to rectify the issue and a link to the appropriate configuration page if applicable.

Top 'access denied' errors

This report shows you the secure pages that visitors have tried to access on the site which they do not have permission to view. Most often, this will be when an anonymous user or unauthenticated site visitor attempts to access the admin areas of the website.

From the main menu, navigate to **Manage | Reports | Top access denied errors**.

Top 'page not found' errors

The page not found report lists the URLs that users tried to access but did not resolve to any content on the Drupal site. Test this by trying to visit a URL that you know doesn't exist: `http://drupal-8.dd:8083/an_unreachable_url`

Note that this report is cleared when you clear the logs from the **Recent log messages** report page.

Top search phrases

The top search phrases report shows a list of the most popular words and phrases searched for using the internal **Drupal Search** (the Search module).

If the Search module is disabled, this report will not appear:

The report shows a list of phrases and how often they have been searched for—you can use this information to better understand how visitors are using your site. Often a search phrase, that is used often, can guide you toward improving the site navigation.

Views plugins

The final default report for the standard installation is the `Views` plugins report. This is a technical report showing all of the available views plugins installed and the views in which they are being used. This is not an everyday use report, but if you are looking to remove a plugin from your site, it's useful to know where it has been utilized so that you can modify the views before removing it. You'll be adding a Views plugin in *Chapter 12, Extending Drupal*.

Summary

We have now had a look at the default reports available in Drupal and how they can benefit you during your site development. We also investigated which other reports become available when optional core modules are enabled.

In the first part of the book, we covered the core of Drupal 8 and what you get "out of the box". In the next section, we will discuss how you can extend Drupal for your own purposes and how you can change the look and feel of your website.

12
Extending Drupal

One of the key strengths of Drupal is the ability to add new modules outside of the core ones that are available to you. There is a huge library of contributed modules available on the drupal.org website that you can download and use for free.

We'll explain how you can install modules you download and also present a few specific modules that are useful across many different types of sites.

Installing a module

Each module has its own project page on drupal.org.

At the bottom of the page will be a list of available versions of the module:

Downloads

Recommended releases

Version	Download	Date
8.x-2.0-rc1	tar.gz (40.67 KB) | zip (59.39 KB)	2015-Nov-22
7.x-2.1	tar.gz (38.72 KB) | zip (45.83 KB)	2014-Nov-29
6.x-4.1	tar.gz (37.5 KB) | zip (43.08 KB)	2014-Nov-29

Development releases

Version	Download	Date
8.x-2.x-dev	tar.gz (40.9 KB) | zip (59.86 KB)	2015-Dec-17
7.x-2.x-dev	tar.gz (39.07 KB) | zip (46.29 KB)	2015-Nov-15
6.x-4.x-dev	tar.gz (37.87 KB) | zip (43.6 KB)	2015-Nov-04

Note that many modules will have supported versions for previous releases of Drupal—you can only use modules with an 8.x version.

Ideally, you will want to use a recommended version of a Drupal 8 release. However, at the time of writing, many modules are still in the development stage, which means they are not recommended for production sites.

Now, we will continue with our example site and try out some different methods of installing new modules, in particular to improve one of the listings — the FAQs.

Improving FAQs

In *Chapter 7, Advanced Content*, you created a page view that represented the list of FAQs as simple clickable questions like this:

Frequently Asked Questions

How can we ensure that we get the most from a
training course?

Now, we are now going to extend Drupal so that we can represent the FAQs page using the commonly used accordions pattern as shown here:

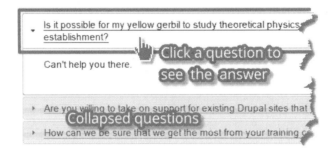

We are first going to download and install a contributed module called `views_accordion`, and then we'll edit the exiting FAQs view to use the new Views Display plugin that the module provides.

Downloading the Views Accordion module

Modules can be downloaded from the Drupal website (`http://www.drupal.org`). The **Views Accordion** project page can be found at:

Installing the module through the UI

We covered the idea of evaluating modules on `drupal.org` back in *Chapter 3, Basic Concepts*, and at the time of writing the Views Accordion module for Drupal did not have a stable release (currently `8.x-1.0-alpha1`). However, we know it works well enough for our purposes here.

Copy the URL of the link to either of the archives:

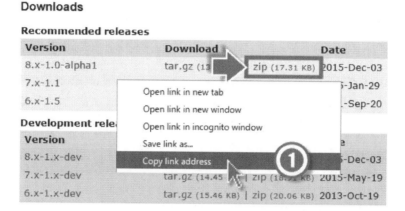

Visit the **Extend** page on your local site and click on **Install new module**:

You will see a momentary modal popup window appear as the module code is downloaded and then you will see a second confirmation page which tells you that the installation was completed successfully.

Click the **Enable newly added modules** link to do just that:

Type a few appropriate letters in the **Search** box to filter down the modules list, then enable the **Views Accordion** checkbox:

In order to see the views_accordion plugin at work, we will need to rework our view as a field-based view rather than a content-teaser view.

Visit your FAQ page at /faq and click on **Edit view** in the contextual links and click the **Content** link in the **Format** section:

Frequently Asked Questions

Narrow down your FAQ search...

- Any -   ▼   ① Edit view

Apply this filter

FORMAT

Format: Unformatted list | Settings

Show: Content | Teaser
Change the way content is formatted.   ②

Then, in the popup window choose **Fields** and click on **Apply (all displays)**:

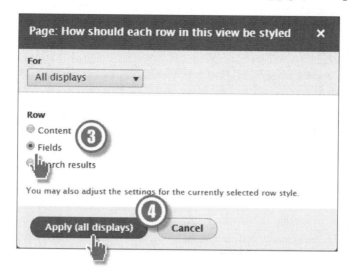

Click on **Apply** one last time and the view will now be field-based.

The view will need two fields active: firstly, the **Title**, which forms the clickable parts of the accordion, and then the **Answer** as the content, that gets revealed—this is, in fact, simply the **Body** field. So, the next step is to add the **Answer** (the **Body** field) into the field list.

To do this, click on the **Add** button (marked as **5** in the following screenshot). Then, type answer into the **Search** input (**6**), so as to narrow down the list of available fields on the left-hand side.

Enable the **Body** field (**7**), and finally hit **Apply (all displays)**:

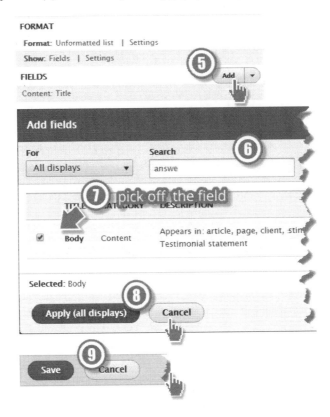

In the subsequent pop-up window, you can leave all settings at default values and click on **Apply (all displays)** again.

Lastly, choose to use the newly provided plugin. Under **Format**, click on the **Unformatted list** link (**1**):

In the resulting pop-up window, choose the **jQuery UI accordion** option (2) and then click on **Apply (all displays)** again (3):

In the subsequent pop-up window, you can leave all the settings at their default values and click on **Apply** one final time.

Lastly, press the **Save** button to make all your changes permanent:

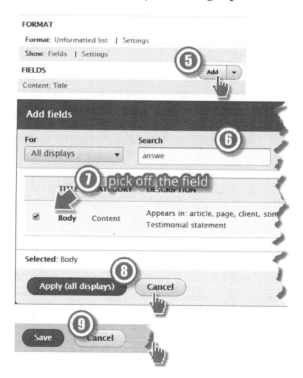

You will see from the Views preview area that the view is now accordion-powered:

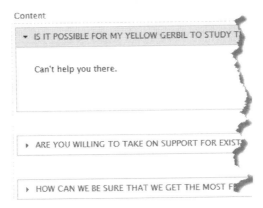

Save the view and return to the FAQ page to see the new accordion-powered view:

Pathauto and Token

Next, we are going to install two modules that work together: Pathauto (drupal.org/project/pathauto) and Token (drupal.org/project/token).

Download, install, and enable both of these modules as earlier. You'll see that Pathauto has a dependency on Token, meaning you cannot use Pathauto until the Token module has also been installed.

Earlier in the book, you'll remember that we specified the URLs of pages as `node/4`, and so on. This is not particularly user friendly, and we saw that the URL of a page can be added manually.

The `Pathauto` module allows you to create patterns for new content URLs so that a standard pattern is created for the content. This is beneficial to your users and also to search engines.

Install both the `Pathauto` and the `Token` module now

Once you have installed both the modules, navigate to:

Configuration | Search and Metadata | URL aliases (`admin/config/search/path`).

You've been here before, but now you'll see additional tabs on this screen, in particular, a **Patterns** tab.

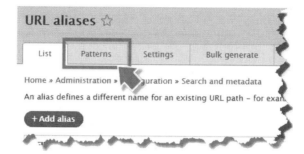

Click on **Patterns** and scroll down to the **CONTENT PATHS** section.

You will see the list of existing content types with any associated patterns. The default pattern is preset:

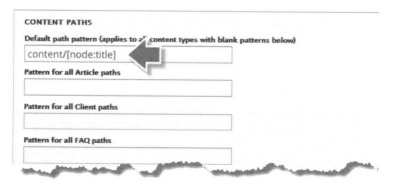

Immediately below the patterns, you can see a list of possible replacement patterns; this is where the `Token` module comes in.

There is a huge array of available tokens you can use:

REPLACEMENT PATTERNS

Click a token to insert it into the field you've last clicked.

NAME	TOKEN	DESCRIPTION
▶ Current date		Tokens related to the current date and time.
▶ Current page		Tokens related to the current page request.
▶ Current user		Tokens related to the currently logged in user
▶ Nodes		Tokens related to individual content items, or
▶ Random		Tokens related to random data.
▶ Site information		Tokens for site-wide settings and other globa

Enter the following path pattern for the Article content type made up of three tokens (refer to the following screenshot):

1. `[node:field_article_type]`
2. `[node:created:custom:Y/m]`
3. `[node:title]`

[node:field_article_type]/[node:created:custom:Y/m]/[node:title]

①　②　③

The idea here is to create a URL in the same shape as those that we specified back in the section entitled *Introducing your site-building scenario* in the early part of *Chapter 5, Basic Content*.

What we have now done is created patterns so that each article created will have a URL that includes the creation date and the title of the article in a URL-friendly format:

1. The first token is replaced with the category of the article: `article`, `blog-post`, or `news`.

2. The second token is replaced with the date of creation of that article in a simple `year-month` format.

3. The third token is replaced by the article title.

All the replacement tokens are also cleaned up, in the sense that they are all converted to lowercase, have spaces, and have some predefined words (`in`, `is`, `that`, `the`, `this`, and `with`) removed.

Try creating a new blog article now entitled `another-blog-article`.

When you view the new article, you should see what would have been the original un-aliased URL (in our case, `node/29`) is now replaced by something that is much more human readable.

http://drupal-8.dd:8083/node/29 ⬇
http://drupal-8.dd:8083/blog-posts/2015-06/another-blog-article

Note that you can still visit `node/29`, since we have only created an alias of it, not replaced it.

Now, go ahead and supply similar patterns for all the content types.

Note the following:

- We removed the `content/` prefix from the **Default path pattern** field.
- We have left the **Pattern for all Basic page paths** field blank, so it will inherit the new default:

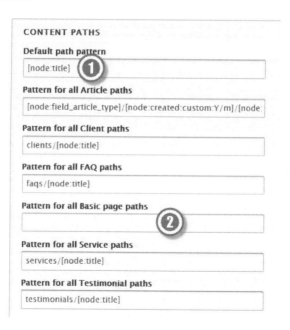

Generating paths from patterns

Creating and editing URL patterns has no retrospective effect on the existing content. However, click on the **Generate** tab, and you'll see there's a way to regenerate all content paths based on the patterns you created.

 Note that this will only work on content with no path already set. If you want to overwrite an old pattern, you will have to use the **Delete aliases** tab first.

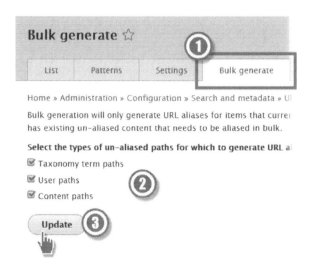

You should now see that all your node paths as seen in your browser address bar are much more friendly, for example, `http://drupal-8.dd:8083/services/drupal-training-courses`.

Pathauto settings

Finally, the settings tab allows you to fine-tune how the URL patterns are generated. We won't go into depth here as there are many options; hopefully, you will find them self-explanatory. From here, you can decide how to handle spaces and non-alphanumeric characters in your paths.

Summary

In this chapter, we introduced some of the key ideas for extending Drupal using some example community or contrib modules that were published on the `drupal.org` website.

We covered improving the FAQs page by installing a Views format plugin that enabled us to present the FAQs as "accordions".

We also covered the use of a couple of key real-life build tools, notably the `Pathauto` and `Token` modules, to provide us with SEO- and human-friendly URL aliases.

13

Theming Drupal

Now that you know how to build a site using the toolkit provided by Drupal 8, it's time to learn how to make it look the part. In this chapter, we will look at applying a design to your website—a process often referred to as **theming**.

In particular, we will look at the themes included in Drupal Core and the differences between them as well as how you can customize them.

Then, we will look at adding new themes from the Drupal community site and extending them to get the results we are looking for.

What is a theme?

The **theme** used for your Drupal site is the design and layout that is applied to the functional site you have built so far.

In other systems you may have used, this could have been described as a "skin" or "design layer". Some might also refer to this as the "look and feel" of the site.

It is possible for you to use one theme for the users of the site and another for the editors, and this is often the case in practice.

There are many themes available for Drupal, and these can make exactly the same Drupal site look very different with the quick change of a setting.

Terminology

A theme can be broken up into *templates*, each of which consists of a number of regions. You will remember from earlier chapters that you place content (for example, blocks) into different theme regions. Each theme you use will define its own regions.

This fact there is a common pattern of region names in all the core themes means that it is often possible to switch between themes without having to change any other settings.

Themes included in Drupal 8

When you install Drupal 8, there are a three themes that are included. These can be classified as:

- Accessible via the UI
- Base themes

Accessible via the UI

These themes are accessible via the user interface.

Bartik

The default Drupal frontend theme, this will be active for all content pages when Drupal is initially installed. It is in fact a subtheme of **Classy** — that is, it is based on or "built on top of" the Classy theme.

Seven

This is the default backend/admin theme. This can also be set as the default frontend theme, but it is really designed to be the common administration theme. This too is a subtheme of Classy.

Stark

This is a very minimal theme that includes the smallest amount of HTML markup and styling. Unlike Bartik and Seven, this theme is not built on top of anything and shows off the raw HTML markup that comes out of modules. As such, it's useful to developers to determine whether module-related CSS and JavaScript are interfering with a more complex theme.

Base themes

These are the base themes.

Classy

Classy is hidden from the UI at **Manage | Appearance** because you are not supposed to use it directly; is designed as a theme on which to base other themes – it is a *base theme*.

Classy is so-named because it presents Drupal's common classes on HTML elements within the mark-up that render on a page.

Both the Bartik and Seven themes are based on Classy.

Stable

The Stable is another hidden theme that is used if you only want to see the stable Drupal core mark-up. Creating your own themes is beyond the scope of this beginners' book but what we will say is that if you make a brand new theme and you don't explicitly tell Drupal that your new theme is based on Classy then the Stable theme is used by default. Themes based on Stable will present much leaner mark-up than those based on Classy.

Setting the active theme

From the **Manage** menu, click on **Appearance**:

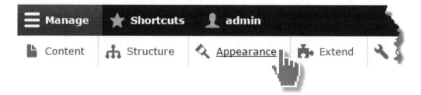

You will then see a list of (visible) themes that are available:

For each theme, you should see a representative example screenshot. If the theme is not the current active theme, you should see a **Set as default** link. Clicking on this will replace the active theme on your site with the new one from the list.

For now, we will continue with Bartik as our default theme as it is the theme most suitable for customizing your site so far without having to write any code.

Common settings

Each theme can provide its own settings, but all themes have a common configuration. Click on the **Settings** link next to the **Bartik** theme to open the available configuration.

For now, skip over (collapse) the **Color scheme** option (we'll come to that later).

Toggle display

Inside the **TOGGLE DISPLAY** menu, you will see a list of checkboxes as follows:

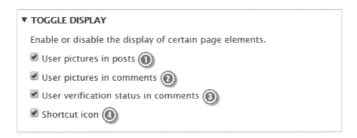

Item	Description
1	If we are opting to show the author information with posted content, if the author has an attached picture, then display it as a small thumbnail icon.
2	If we are opting to show author information with posted comments and the comment author has an attached picture, then display it as a small thumbnail icon.
3	User verification status in comments.
4	Use a shortcut icon also known as the `favicon.ico`. Defaults to the drop.

By default, if the theme you have chosen to use includes its own `logo.svg` (Scalable Vector Graphic) file then that will be used as the logo.

The default logo is a semi-transparent version of the Drupal 'drop' character:

Thus, when used overlaying the Bartik's theme blue header, it appears:

If you choose to un-tick the **Use the default logo supplied by the theme** option then you are given the chance to point to, or upload, an alternative.

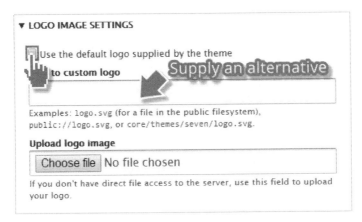

The default shortcut icon, often referred to as the favicon, is also the Drupal drop icon.

Once again, if you would like to replace it with something else then the option is there.

Theme regions

To see an onscreen preview of the Regions within the Bartik theme, visit the **Block layout** page:

Check that you are on the Bartik page and click **Demonstrate block regions (Bartik)**:

There are 17 named regions in the Bartik theme depicted slightly differently to what you are currently seeing so as to make their names a bit more readable on the printed page:

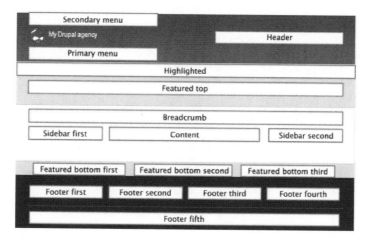

To exit the preview display, click on the **Exit block region demonstration** link:

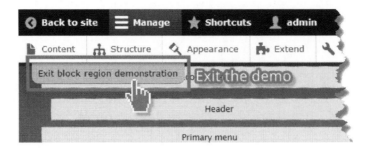

Color scheme

If you enable the optional **Color** module (enabled by default in a standard installation), it is possible to change the color scheme of some themes. Note that not all themes support this, but the default Bartik theme does.

Go back to the **Appearance** page and select **Settings** for the Bartik theme.

At the top of the page (collapsed earlier), you will then see the following:

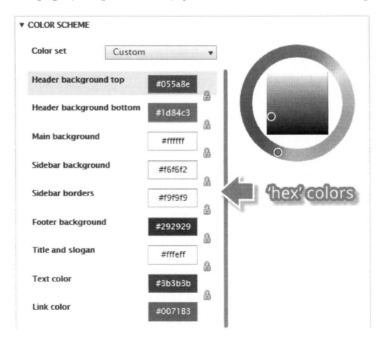

There are a number of preset color sets that work together—you can select these from the **Color set** dropdown. The default theme is called **Blue Lagoon**. If you don't like the defaults or have some specific theme in mind, you can change the colors of individual components manually by selecting **Custom** from the dropdown and then clicking on each of the color fields to set the hexadecimal number values to match any existing designs.

Alternatively, you can click on the color selector wheel to the right when you have focused on a specific field to automatically fill in the value.

Setting the admin theme

The theme you use when editing your site is not necessarily the same as the one users see when they are browsing your site. Drupal 8 includes a specially designed admin theme.

Go back to the **Appearance** page:

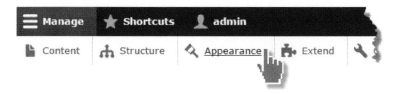

At the bottom of the appearance page is a panel allowing you to specify the **Administration theme**:

The checkbox underneath the theme selection allows you to specify which themes (the frontend theme or the admin theme) are used when the content is being edited.

As a rule, using the administration theme will give you a better editing experience.

Advanced themes from the Drupal community

The Drupal community is starting to publish a number of Drupal 8 compliant themes on the drupal.org site. We'll take a look now at one such theme and how you can download, install, and use it to restyle your site.

Installing a new theme

From the main menu, click on **Appearance** and then click on **Install new theme**:

In our example, we will download the popular Bootstrap theme from drupal.org and then copy the theme to the correct place in our installation before installing it. Go to https://www.drupal.org/project/bootstrap and install the latest version:

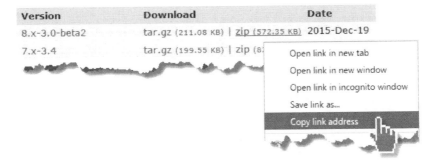

Enter the URL of the project from drupal.org just as you did when you installed new modules back in *Chapter 12, Extending Drupal*.

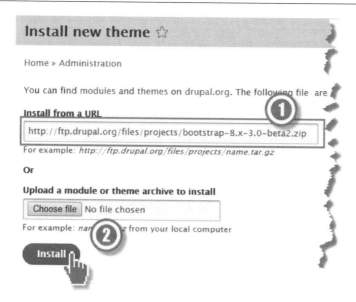

The theme will be physically downloaded into the themes folder and will then be available for installation on the Appearance page.

Locate the new theme on the page and click **Install and set as default** theme:

Uninstalled theme

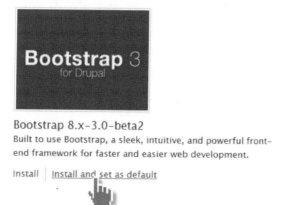

Bootstrap is actually a public frontend framework released by the Twitter team (http://getbootstrap.com/). This theme is a Drupal implementation of the Bootstrap framework, and you may recognize some styles from the other websites you have used.

If you don't want to create your own bespoke theme, Bootstrap is a great way to give your website a professional look and gives you a great deal of scope for customization using theme settings.

Here is a screenshot of what the **Contact** form looks like when viewed in the newly applied theme:

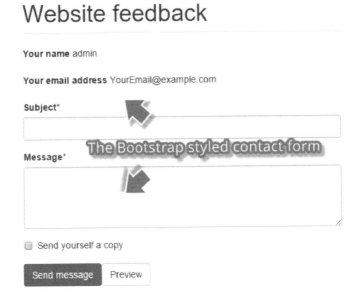

The Bootstrap styled contact form

Now, go back to the settings page, and you will see a huge array of settings that were not available with the Bartik theme.

There are too many to go through in detail here, and it's quite likely there will be even more by the time you read this. So for the purpose of this chapter, we'll just point out where those settings appear and leave you to explore the effect of them on your site:

Bootstrap Settings

▼ **GENERAL**

   ▼ **BUTTONS**

     ☑ Colorize Buttons
       Adds classes to buttons based on their text value.
       See also: Buttons, hook_bootstrap_colorize_text_alter()

     ☑ Iconize Buttons
       Adds icons to buttons based on the text value
       See also: hook_bootstrap_ic

     Default button size

     | Normal ▼ |

     Normal
     Extra Small
     Small
     Large

Highly configurable via the UI

This should give you an idea of how much you can do through configuration of a Drupal theme without actually having to create your own from scratch.

Custom themes

If you are working on a website for commercial use, it's probable that you will have designs or at least design guidelines to follow. It is possible to create your own custom themes for Drupal to achieve the exact look and feel you need.

Creating custom themes is beyond the scope of this book, but before we conclude this topic, it's worth introducing a couple of other concepts important to Drupal theming when you take the next step.

Base themes and subthemes

Drupal themes are designed to be extendible so that you can build a theme of your own that only changes some small aspects of a parent theme. It's not best practice to edit the content of any part of Drupal core, but you may, for example, want to modify the CSS of the Bartik theme for your own purposes.

In this scenario, you would make a subtheme of the Bartik theme and then edit the CSS in your version of the theme. As mentioned earlier, some of the other themes provided in Drupal core such as Classy is not designed to be used directly, but are intended to be the Base theme for you to build on top of.

In the same way, you would not edit the contents of these themes in Drupal core. In order to make a change to their design, you would create a subtheme of one of these in the custom theme folder and continue your work in this area.

Summary

In this chapter, we introduced some of the key ideas for applying a different look and feel to your website by switching themes.

We looked at the region architecture provided by the Bartik theme and we experimented with making small theme adjustments via the UI including toggling display elements such as Title and Logo, and color schemes.

We re-themed your Drupal site using the Bootstrap community theme that was published on the `drupal.org` website and we saw how such themes can provide some significant configuration tools via the administrative UI.

14
Getting Support

We have now reached the end of the instructional part of the book. However, Drupal 8 is an extensive software framework and you should not expect to find all of the answers in a "learning" book. In the following chapter, we discuss how the open source Drupal Community works and how you can engage with the community to get help and support for your Drupal project.

In particular, we will cover the following topics:

- What is open source and how does the Drupal Community work together?
- How can you report bugs and request changes?
- Where else can you find help?
- How can you help?

What is open source?

The dictionary definition of open source is:

> *denoting software for which the original source code is made freely available and may be redistributed and modified.*

> *– New Oxford American Dictionary*

While there are no license fees associated with Drupal, the most important part is the fact that you are free to modify and extend the code base to meet your own needs.

Open source means that you can also see the full history of the code—you can see when changes were made, for what reason, and by whom. There is no "black box" technology—everything is open for you to investigate if you desire to.

The Drupal community

One of the key benefits of using Drupal is the community behind the software. Drupal 8 represents the freely donated time of thousands of individuals and companies. The ethos of the community is giving back, and you will find that there are many people willing to help you get the most out of Drupal.

Many people are very successfully using Drupal for their projects without any involvement in the community. However, should you choose to, there are plenty of ways you can find help and support.

Drupal.org

The central location of the Drupal project is the main website, that is, `Drupal.org`. Every Drupal module has its own project page, run by the module maintainer. Each module page explains the purpose of the project and contains links to further documentation.

The following screenshot is from the popular **Rules** module:

On the right-hand side bar, you can find the following:

- **Maintainer**: This is the developer who is responsible for the code and documentation of this module.

- **Co-maintainers**: There are some larger and more complex modules that have multiple maintainers who have permission to update the code.

- **Links to commits**: As all of Drupal is open source, you can see the history of all the files that make up the project. Every change to every file is visible in a commit log, so you can see what was changed and why.

- **Links to issue queues**: This consists of every support question or bug that has been raised for this module.

- **Links to documentation**

- **Change records**: When a change to a module is more significant than a bug fix and may need some action on your part in order to upgrade, a change record is created.

Issue queues

For **Drupal core** and all Drupal contributed modules there is an issue queue, which you can use to request support or provide feedback. This is the most reliable way of communicating with the maintainers of the modules in question.

Remember, those individuals looking after different modules have assumed the responsibility of responding to questions in the issue queues, but they are still volunteers. Some more popular modules generate more questions than it would be possible to process as a full-time job.

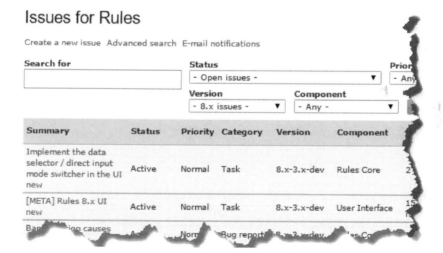

Reporting a bug or requesting support

If you want to communicate with the module maintainer or Drupal core team, create a new issue using the project page.

In order to get attention for your issue, be as clear and descriptive as possible. If you are reporting a bug, provide the steps to reproduce it.

The best practice for getting help in the Drupal issue queues is as follows:

1. Always search first, in case someone has experienced the problem before.
2. Be clear and descriptive when you file an issue.
3. Try to include steps to reproduce the problem if you are reporting a bug.
4. Be considerate of the module owner in the phrasing you use—these are volunteers giving up their own time.

5. Do not reopen an old issue if it has been closed for a long period of time.

6. Think carefully about the priority you set—just because it is your number one priority does not mean it will be for other users.

7. If you think you have a solution to the issue you are reporting, suggest it or, even better, attach a patch file that fixes it.

The Drupal security team

If you come across an issue in Drupal core or in a contributed module that you think is a potential security risk for other users, there is a slightly different process. If there is a genuine vulnerability, it is best to report it privately to the Drupal security team who will work with the module maintainer to resolve it if necessary.

When a fix is available, a security notification is sent out explaining the vulnerability and the mitigating factors involved.

There is a special link to report a security issue on all module pages:

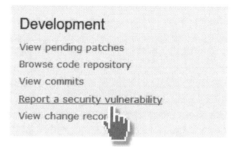

api.drupal.org

The developer documentation for Drupal can be found at api.drupal.org. If you are not carrying out any custom development, you may not need to go there, but if you are working on a custom module or theme, this is an essential reference for every internal function within Drupal.

IRC chat

A popular place to find help is to use **Internet Relay Chat (IRC)**. Many members of the Drupal community can be found in Drupal-specific chat rooms and may be able to offer assistance when you need it.

There are some general channels such as `#drupal` and some very specific channels where groups meet to discuss their areas of interest. You may find `#drupal-support`, a useful channel if you need help.

The Drupal Association

The **Drupal Association** (or **DA** as it is often referred to) is a not-for-profit organization that looks after the interests of the Drupal Community.

You can become a member of the association as an individual or a company, and the membership fees go toward maintaining the infrastructure of `drupal.org` as well as other educational and promotional initiatives. The association is also directly involved in organizing the annual Drupal conference known as *DrupalCon*.

DrupalCon

One of the key events in the Drupal community calendar is the annual *DrupalCon*. Historically, there is one event in North America and one in Europe each year, and more recently, there are events being arranged in South America and Asia.

The North American event attracts 3500-4000 delegates, and the European event attracts over 2000. These events are an opportunity for core and contributed module developers to meet and work together in person. The conference usually lasts a week with a day of training followed by 2 days of presentations in multiple topic tracks. After this, there are traditionally code sprints where community members work together on areas of interest improving the Drupal code base.

To fully understand the Drupal community, it is highly recommended to attend one of these conferences. Here, you will experience the passion and enthusiasm of the community, and if our experience is anything to go by, feel very welcome.

Many of the Drupal development companies and agencies sponsor these events, so it is also a good place to meet prospective employers.

DrupalCamps

By contrast, **DrupalCamps** are much smaller, locally organized events. Depending on the location, these can be small groups of enthusiasts meeting in the local pub or conferences with as many as 1000 delegates (for example, DrupalCamp London or NYCamp in New York).

There are also specialist camps such as FrontEnd United, which focuses on the Drupal theme layer, and DevDays, which is more focused on back end and core development.

The **Drupical** website (`http://www.drupical.com`) is a community project, which maps the locations of upcoming Drupal events.

Specialist Drupal companies

If the needs of your project are more extensive, there are many companies around the world that specialize in Drupal development. The authors of this book both work for **iKOS**—a company specializing in e-commerce with Drupal.

The largest of these organizations is **Acquia**, which was founded by the original developer of Drupal, Dries Buytaert. Acquia's mission is to promote Drupal to the enterprise market.

Other specialist companies such as **Commerce Guys** are dedicated to the development of the Drupal commerce platform.

Training

Some people are very successful at teaching themselves using books such as this, others prefer a classroom-led approach. There are many Drupal training courses offered around the world from beginners "Drupal from Scratch" courses to intensive boot camp style courses.

Certification

There is no officially recognized certification for Drupal development like there is for many other technologies. However, recently Acquia announced their own certification program which is becoming quite popular.

Summary

Drupal is a complex software platform, and while you may experience no problems at all when you build your first website, you may need to reach out for help. The Drupal Community is a very welcoming place, and you should be able to find the help you are looking for through one of the many channels discussed here.

As with any technology, there are no stupid questions. It's important to remember that everyone is learning all the time, and Drupal itself is evolving every day.

Enjoy building your projects with Drupal and come back to this book as reference when you need to. There are lots of people in the community ready and willing to lend a hand if you need them.

Index

O

OpenAtrium 16
OpenPublic 16
OpenScholar 16
open source community
  about 285
  working 10
or tags
  versus fixed terms 35

P

page
  about 67
  adding, to main navigation menu 73, 74
page not found report 255
pager
  adding, to view 139-141
Pantheon
  about 15
  URL 15
Pathauto
  about 264-267
  URL 264
patterns
  paths, generating from 268
People page
  control, taking of 218
performance settings page, development
    section
  about 181
  bandwidth optimization 183
  caching 182
  clear cache 182
permissions
  about 37, 208
  typical roles 210
  typical scenario 211, 212
  user accounts, creating 213-215
personal contact form 53
placeholder text 119, 120
plugins 25
posts 67, 68

R

Really Simple Syndication (RSS) 203-205
Recent log messages report
  about 249, 250
  log details 250, 251
  log messages, filtering 251, 252
  logs, clearing 252
regional settings
  about 200
  locale 200
  time zones 201
reports
  accessing 247, 248
Responsive image module 239-241
responsiveness
  about 45
  administration theme 46
  contextual links 46, 47
retrospective action
  about 83
  comments, previewing before posting 84
  reply form, displaying on same page as
    comments 84
  threading 83
roles
  about 37, 38, 207
  administrator 38, 208
  anonymous user 38
  authenticated user 38

S

search and metadata section
  about 193
  default indexing settings 195
  indexing progress 194
  indexing throttle 194
  logging 195
  search pages 196-198
  URL Aliases 198-200
search engine optimization (SEO) 71
Service content type
  creating 141

Thank you for buying
Learning Drupal 8

About Packt Publishing

Packt, pronounced 'packed', published its first book, *Mastering phpMyAdmin for Effective MySQL Management*, in April 2004, and subsequently continued to specialize in publishing highly focused books on specific technologies and solutions.

Our books and publications share the experiences of your fellow IT professionals in adapting and customizing today's systems, applications, and frameworks. Our solution-based books give you the knowledge and power to customize the software and technologies you're using to get the job done. Packt books are more specific and less general than the IT books you have seen in the past. Our unique business model allows us to bring you more focused information, giving you more of what you need to know, and less of what you don't.

Packt is a modern yet unique publishing company that focuses on producing quality, cutting-edge books for communities of developers, administrators, and newbies alike. For more information, please visit our website at www.packtpub.com.

About Packt Open Source

In 2010, Packt launched two new brands, Packt Open Source and Packt Enterprise, in order to continue its focus on specialization. This book is part of the Packt Open Source brand, home to books published on software built around open source licenses, and offering information to anybody from advanced developers to budding web designers. The Open Source brand also runs Packt's Open Source Royalty Scheme, by which Packt gives a royalty to each open source project about whose software a book is sold.

Writing for Packt

We welcome all inquiries from people who are interested in authoring. Book proposals should be sent to author@packtpub.com. If your book idea is still at an early stage and you would like to discuss it first before writing a formal book proposal, then please contact us; one of our commissioning editors will get in touch with you.

We're not just looking for published authors; if you have strong technical skills but no writing experience, our experienced editors can help you develop a writing career, or simply get some additional reward for your expertise.

Drupal 7 Cookbook

ISBN: 978-1-84951-796-6   Paperback: 324 pages

Over 70 recipes that will advance your Drupal skills from novice to pro

1. Install, set up, and manage a Drupal site and discover how to get the most out of creating and displaying content.

2. Become familiar with creating new content types and use them to create and publish content using Views, Blocks, and Panels.

3. Learn how to work with images, documents, and video and how to integrate them with Facebook, Twitter, and Add this.

Drupal 7 First Look

ISBN: 978-1-84951-122-3   Paperback: 288 pages

Learn the new features of Drupal 7, how they work and how they will impact you

1. Get to grips with all of the new features in Drupal 7.

2. Upgrade your Drupal 6 site, themes, and modules to Drupal 7.

3. Explore the new Drupal 7 administration interface and map your Drupal 6 administration interface to the new Drupal 7 structure.

Please check **www.PacktPub.com** for information on our titles

[PACKT] open source ✻
PUBLISHING community experience distilled

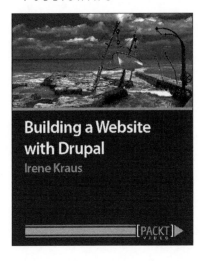

Building a Website with Drupal
Irene Kraus

Building a Website with Drupal [Video]

ISBN: 978-1-78216-614-6   Duration: 02:27 hours

Get hands-on expertise with this comprehensive tutorial on Drupal

1. Watch how a community-oriented website including a forum and blog is built using a test server through actual deployment.

2. Learn how to add fields to existing content types and how to create new ones to match the requirements for a site.

3. Explore views and more to enhance your site and learn how to build page templates without writing any PHP code.

Drupal 7 Module Development
Trevor James

Drupal 7 Module Development [Video]

ISBN: 978-1-78216-118-9   Duration: 03:06 hours

A complete guide to practically building a fully functional custom Drupal 7 module from scratch

1. Use the essential hooks and functions in your module code to build your own custom Drupal 7 module.

2. Create database tables, write database queries and finally build and theme blocks using powerful hook functions.

3. Set up an ideal development environment by reviewing the module from a security and performance standpoint.

Please check **www.PacktPub.com** for information on our titles

Printed in Great Britain
by Amazon